Animals & Birds Coloring Book

This Book Belongs To ....

_____

_____

_____

_____

_____

_____

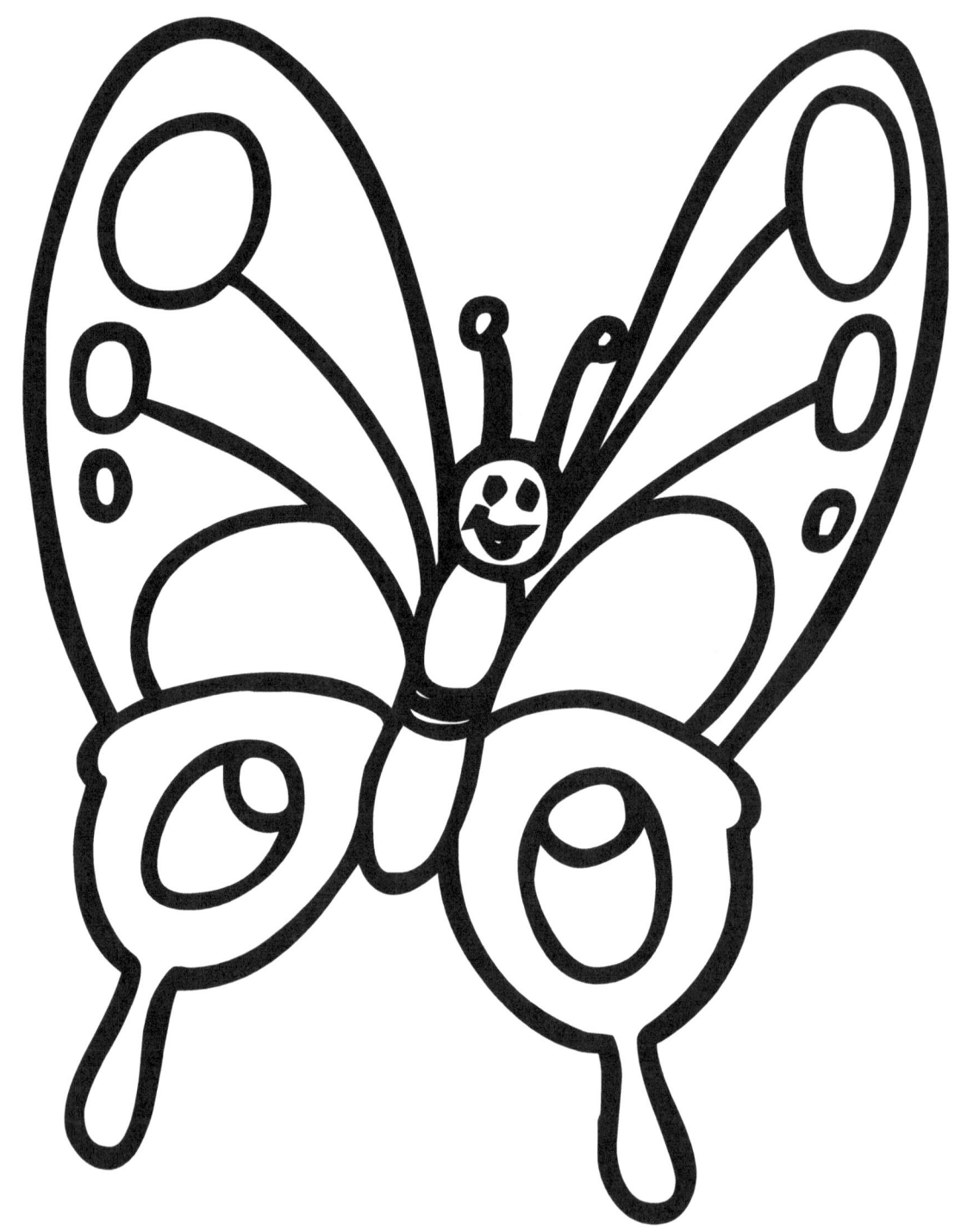

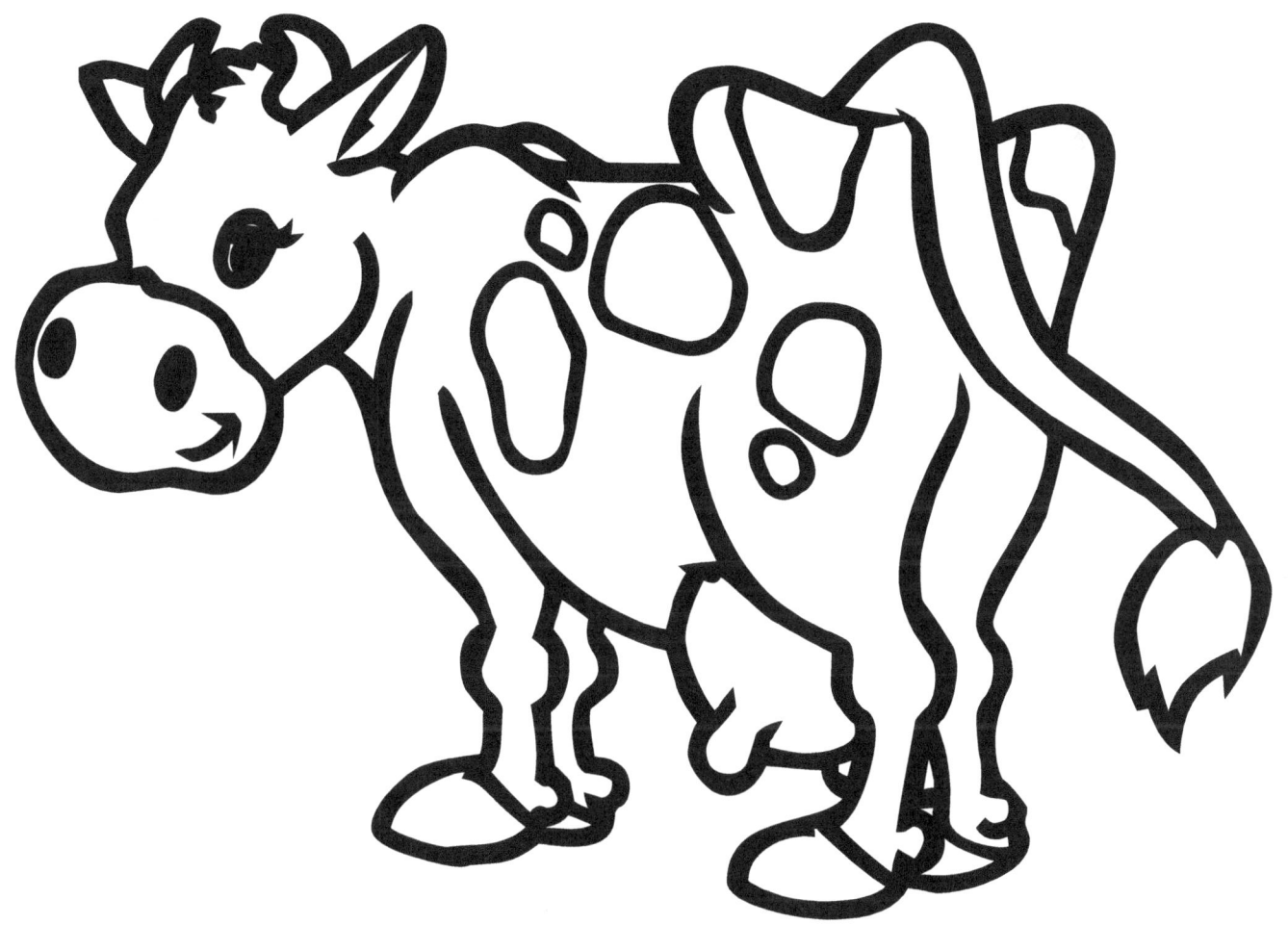

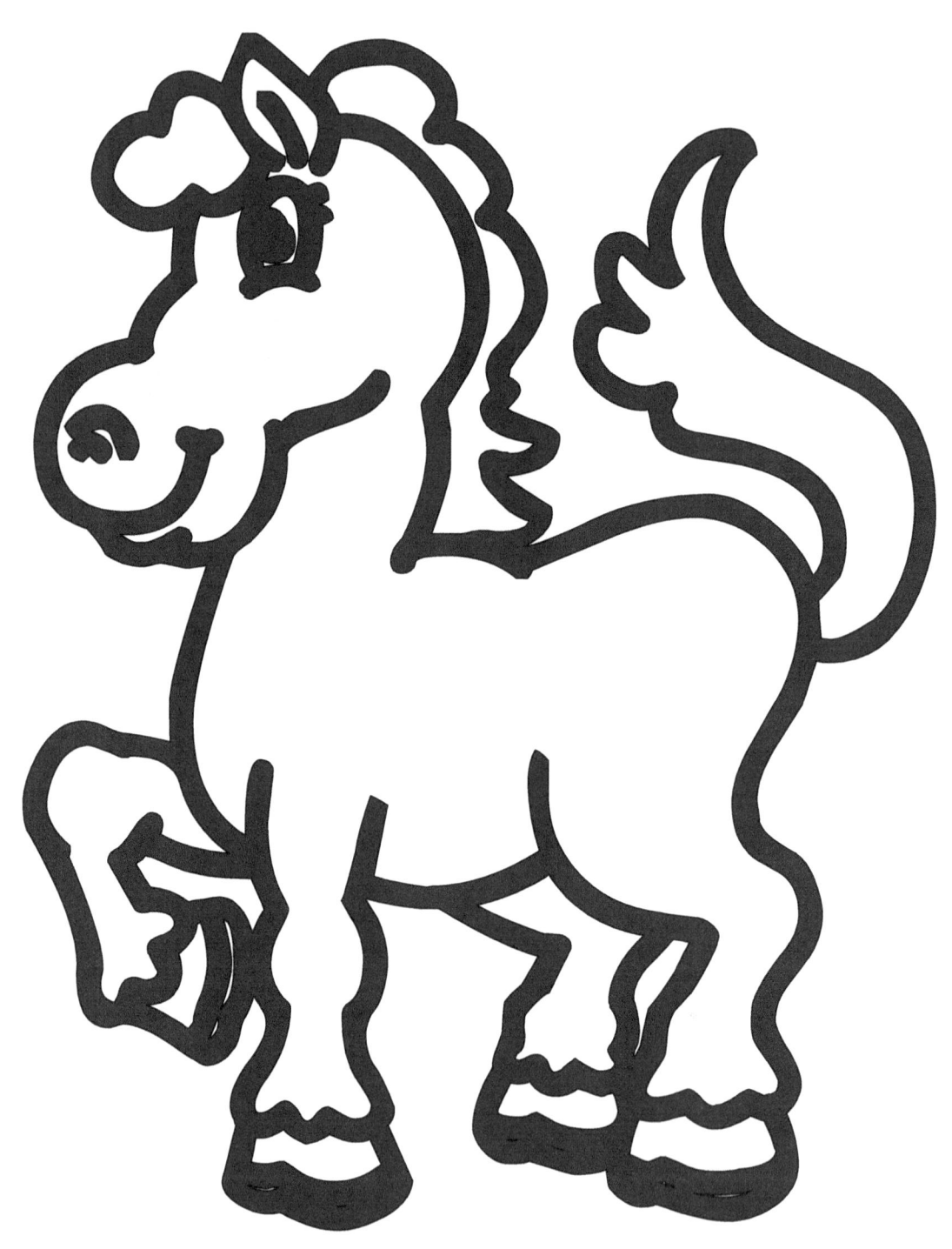

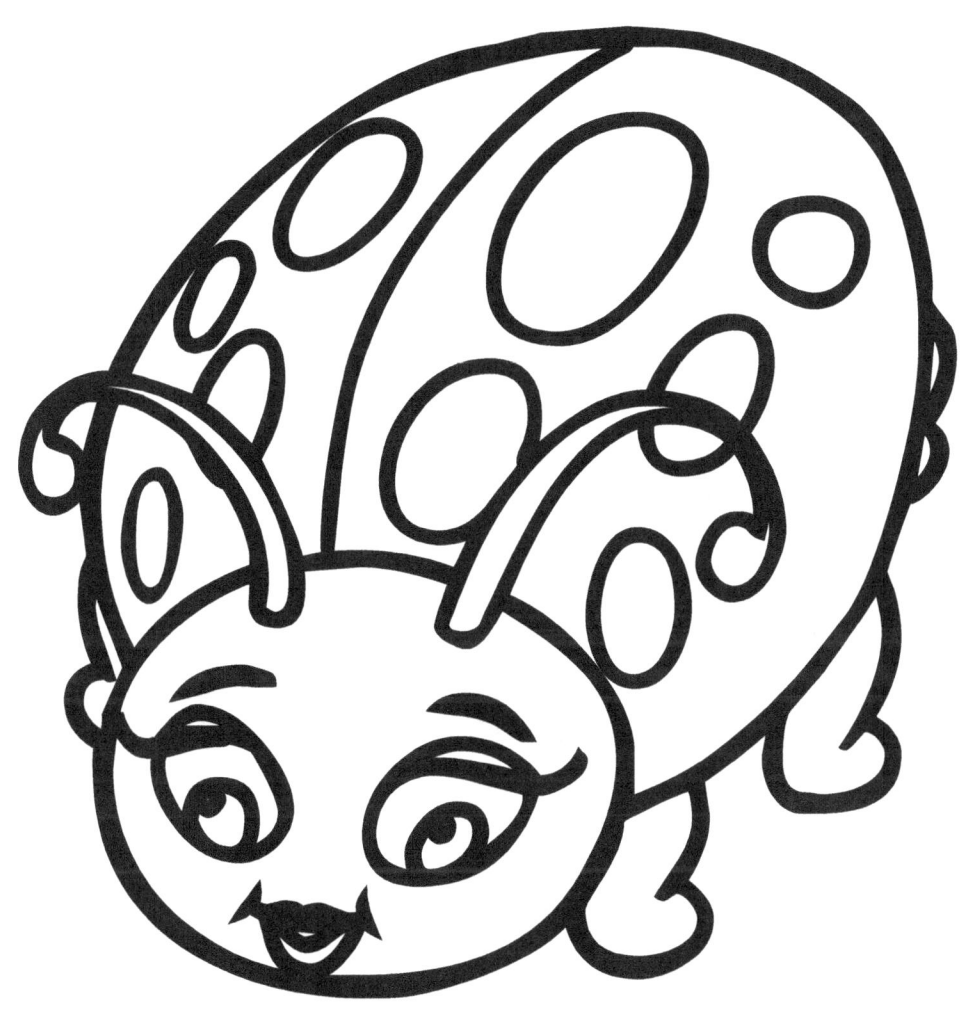

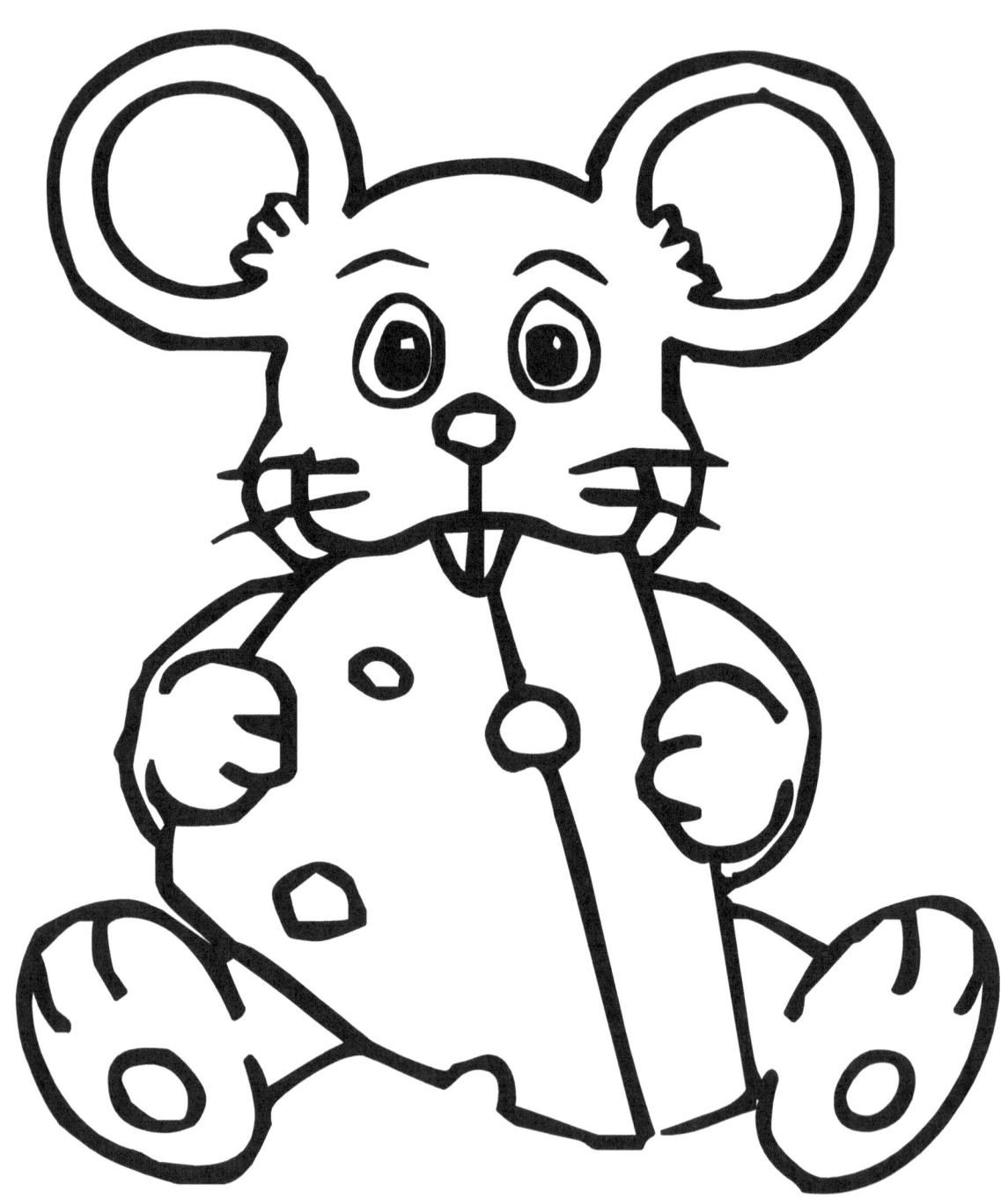

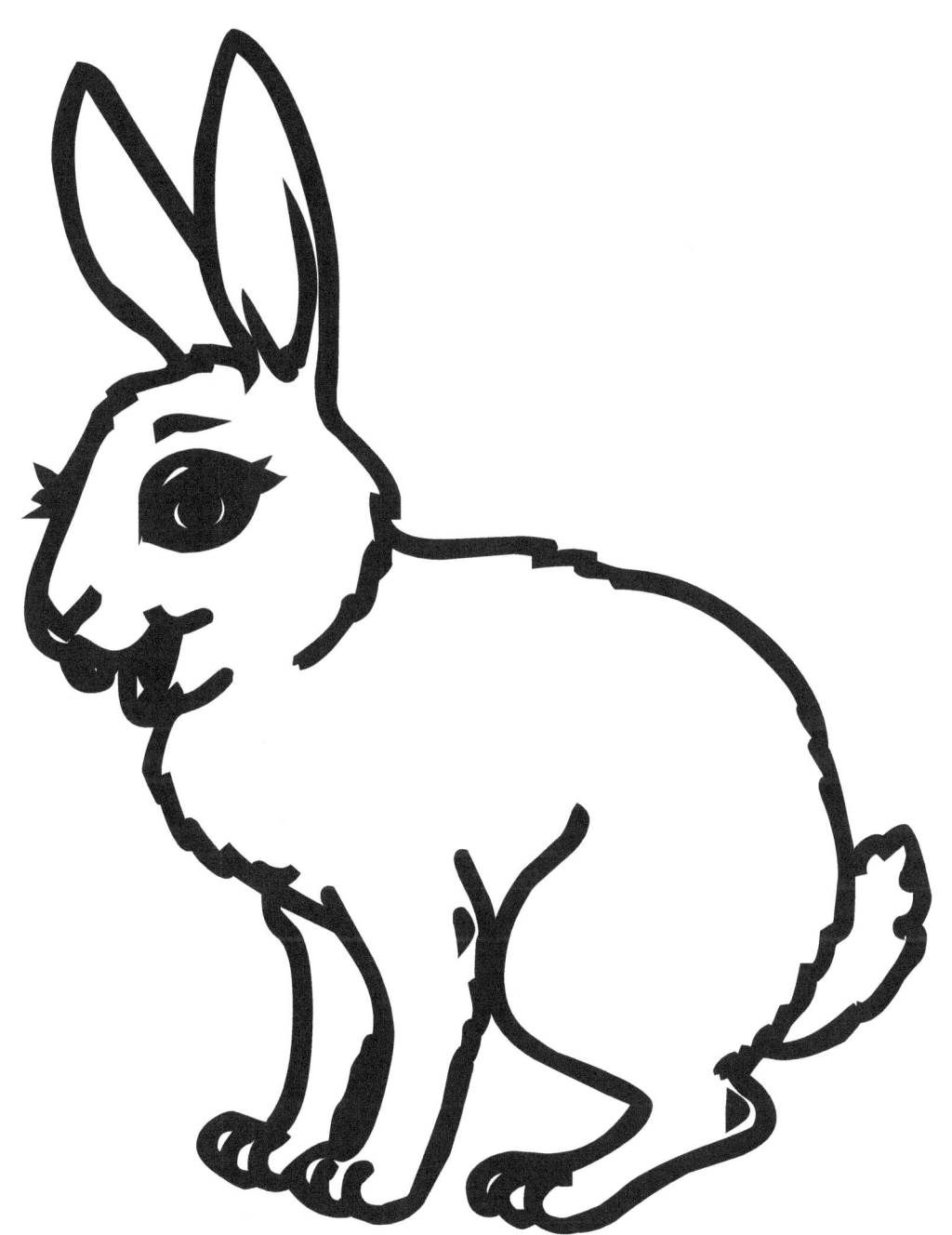

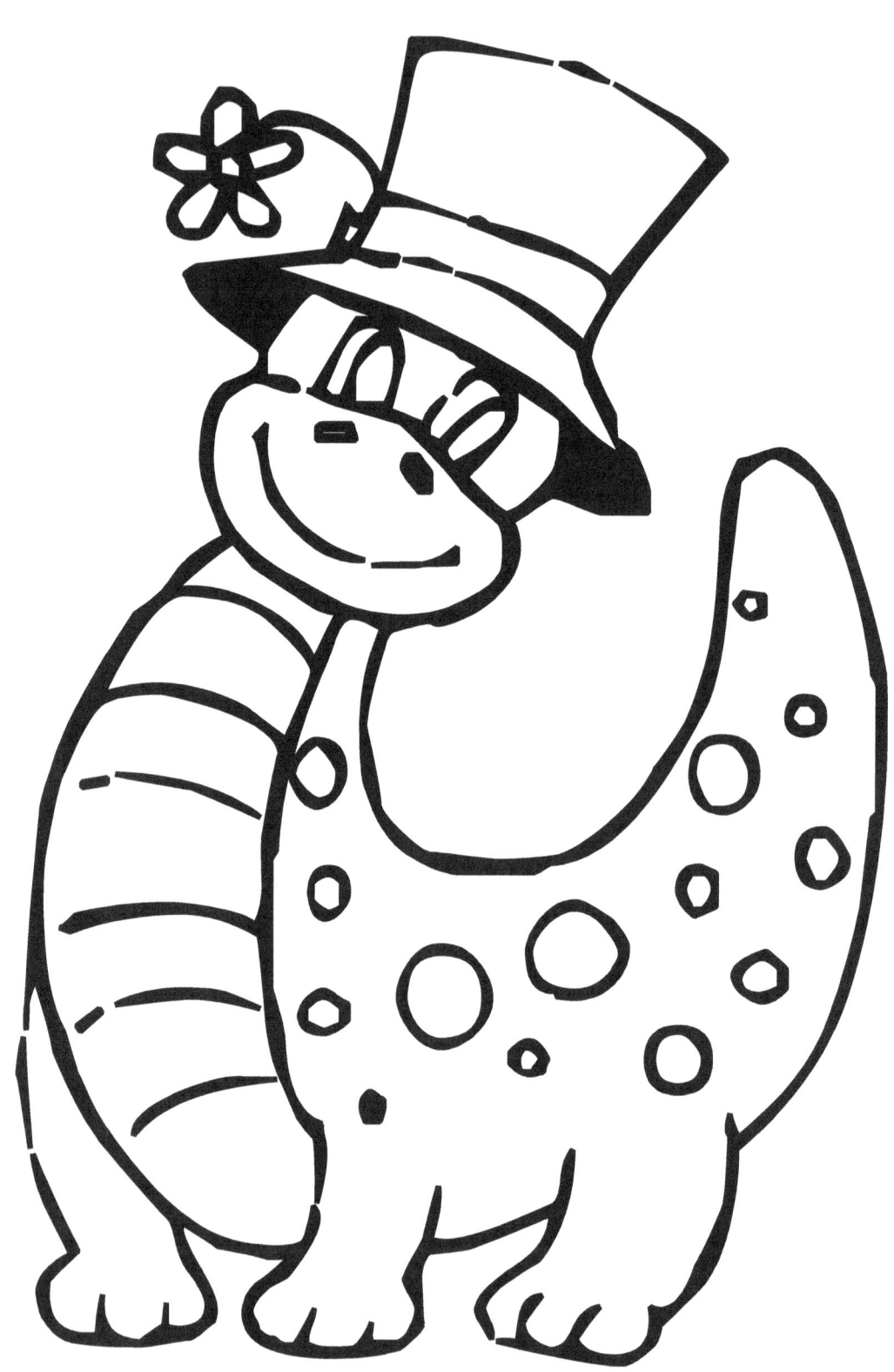

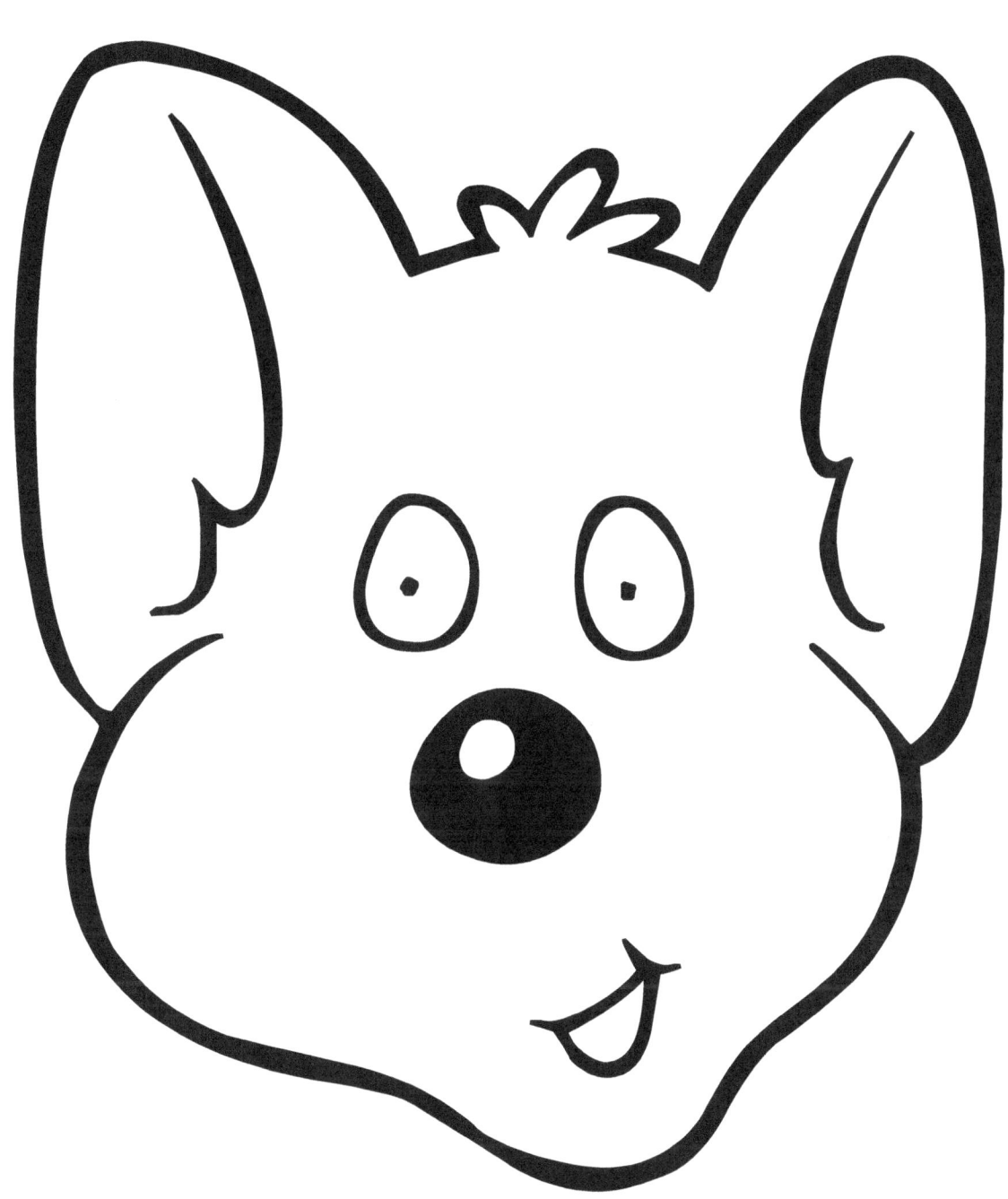

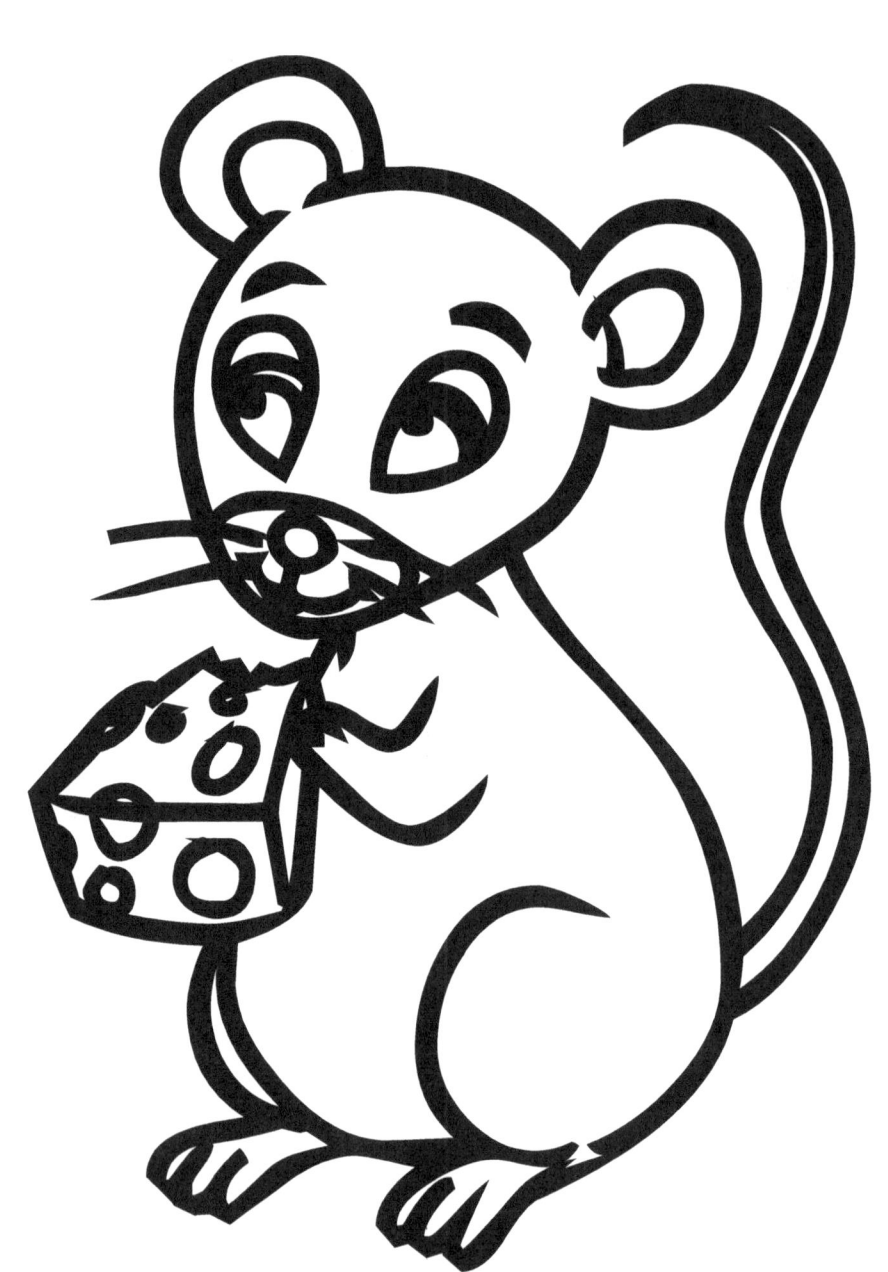

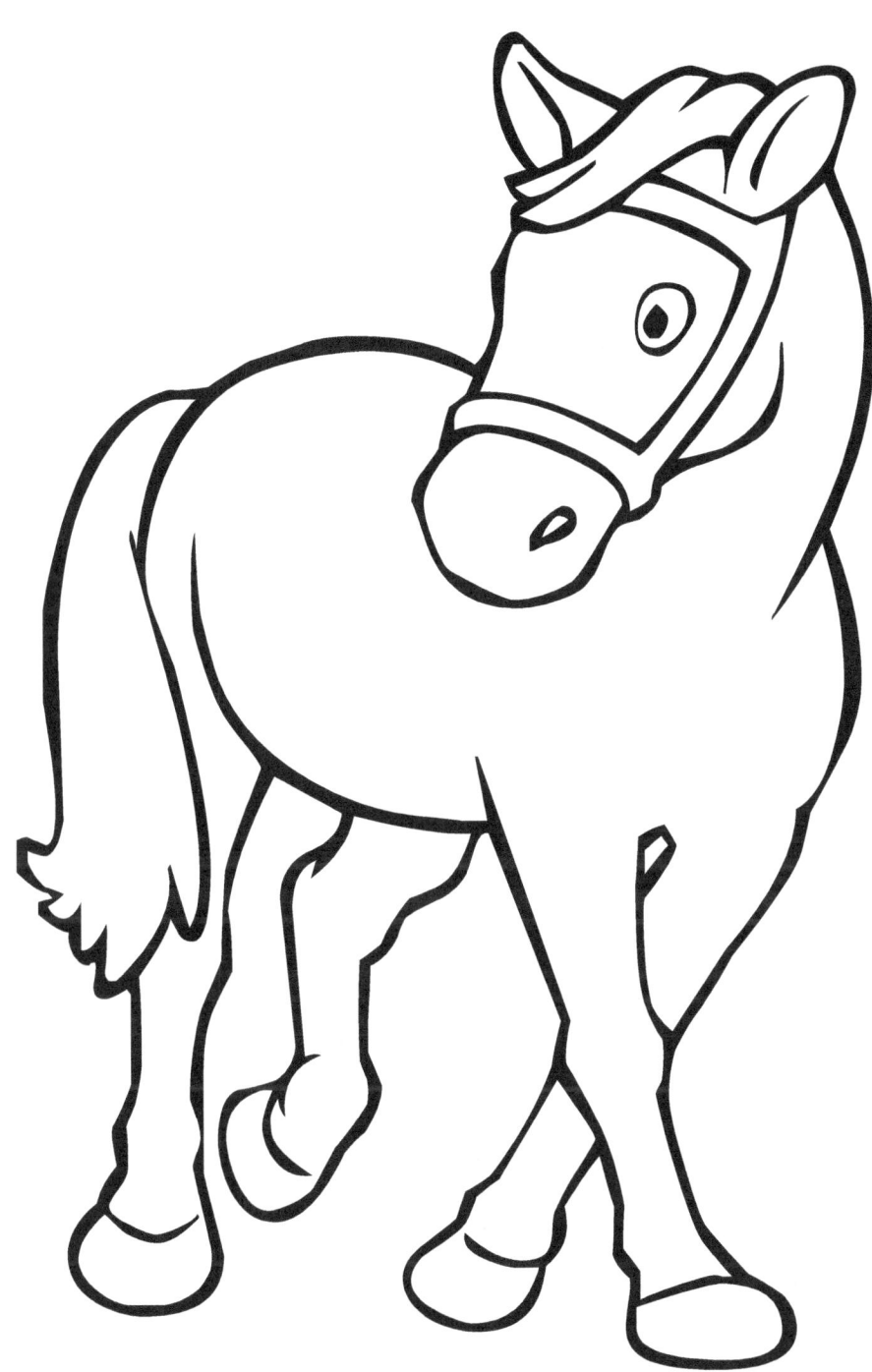

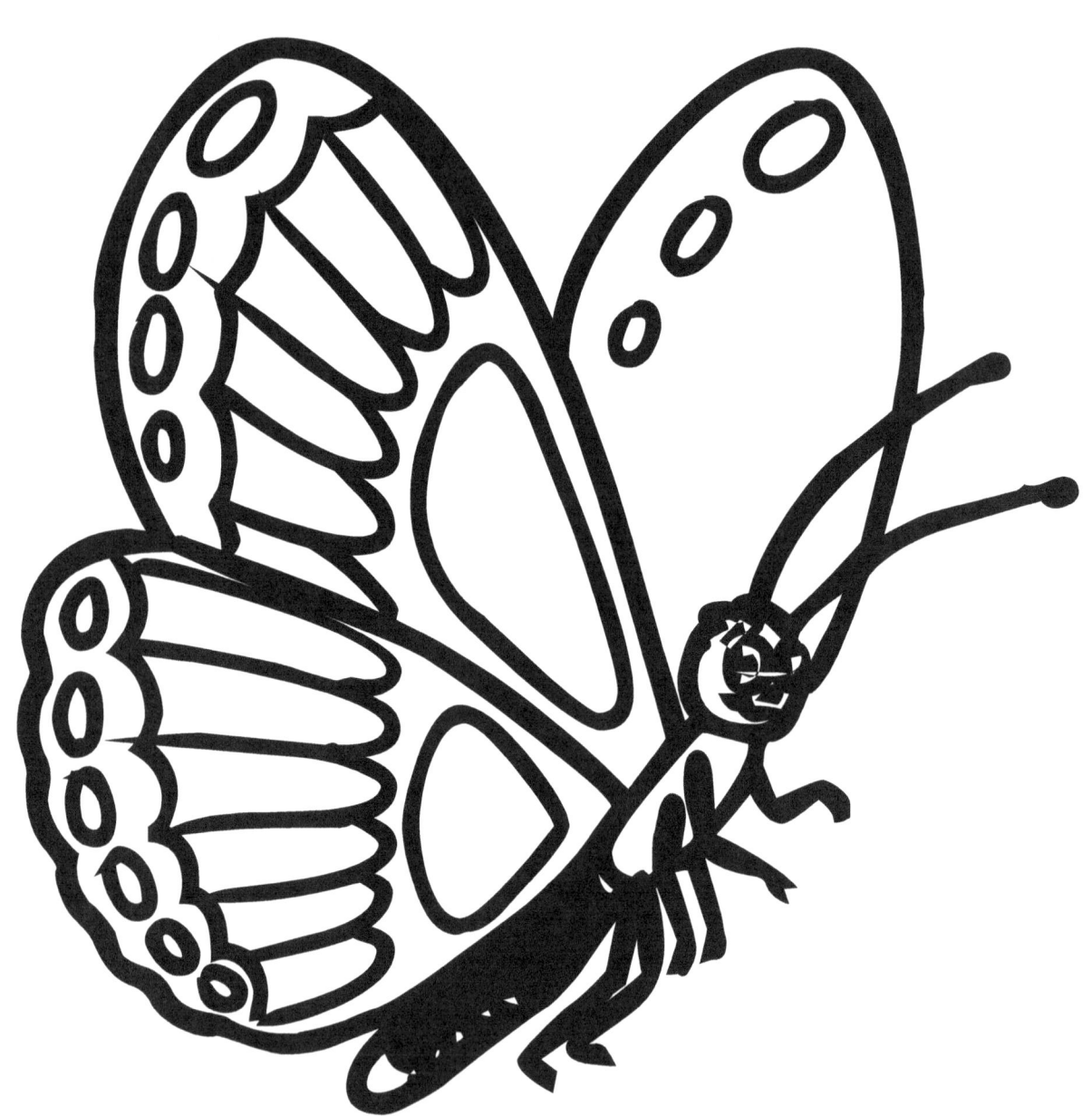

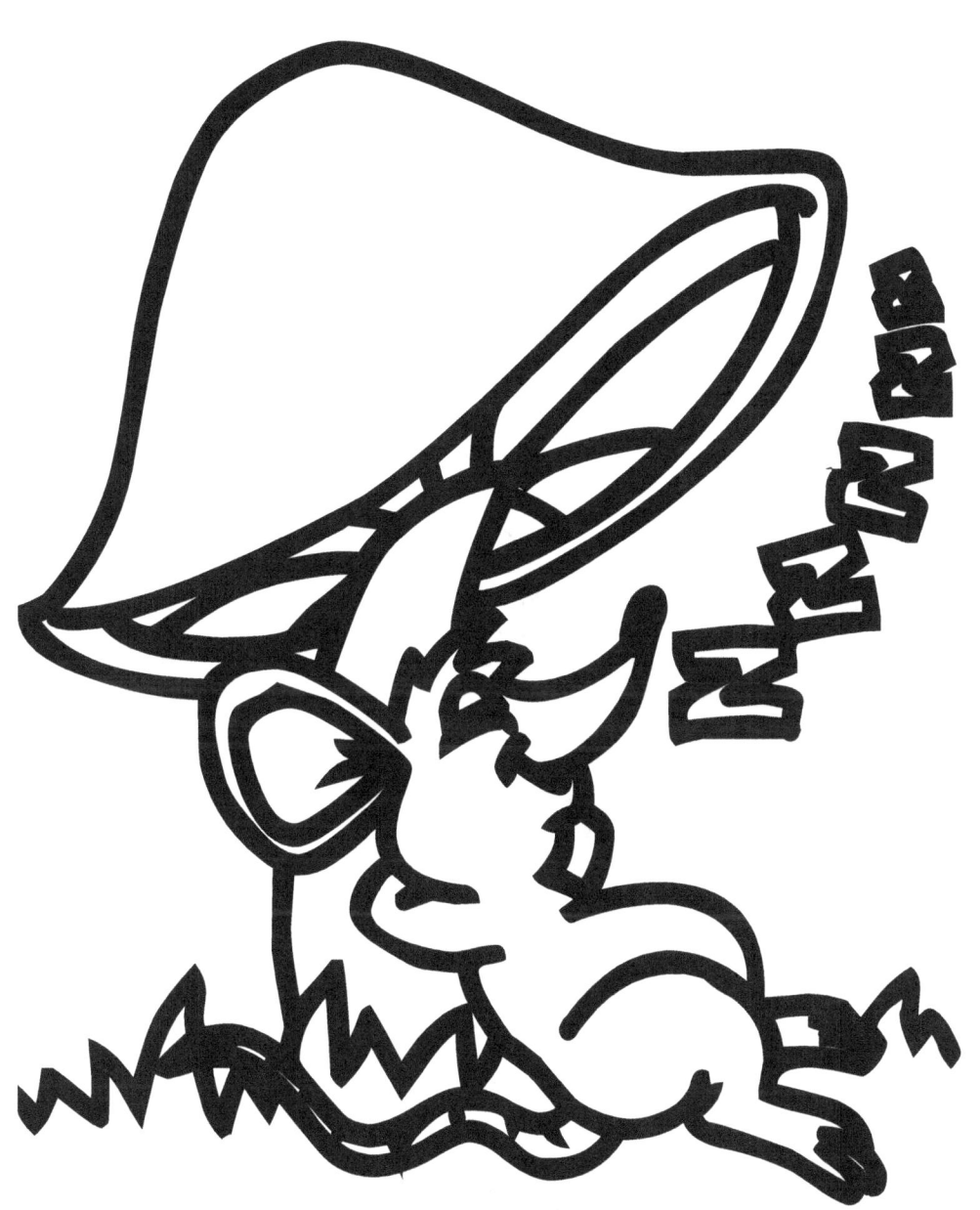

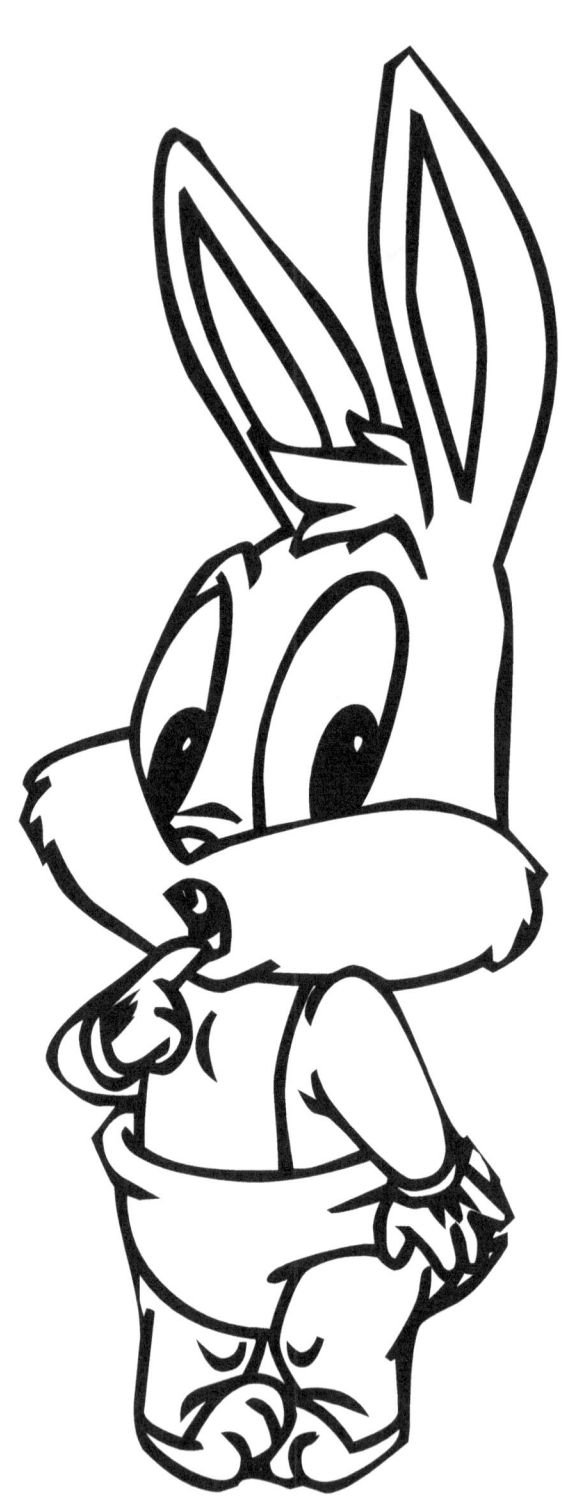

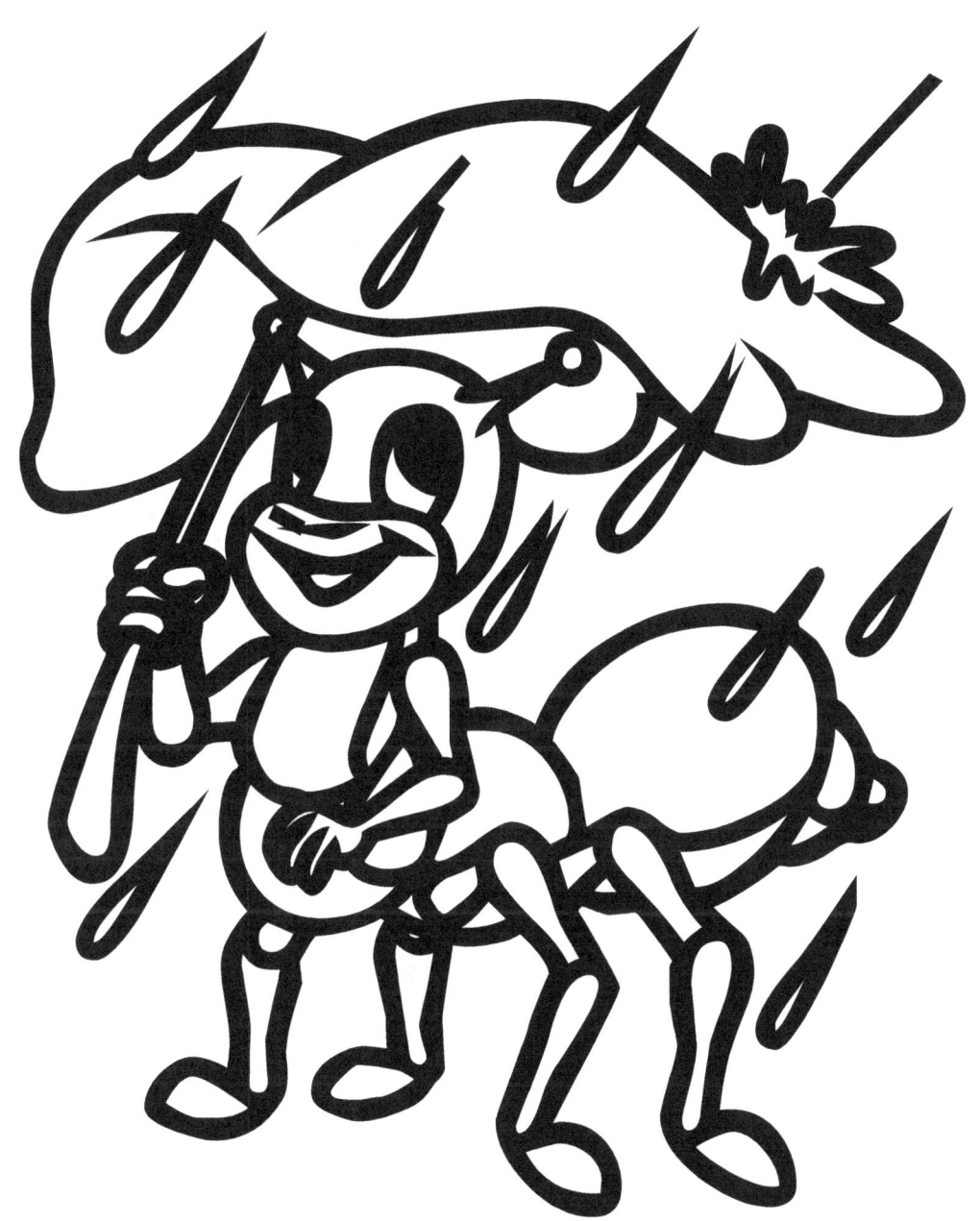

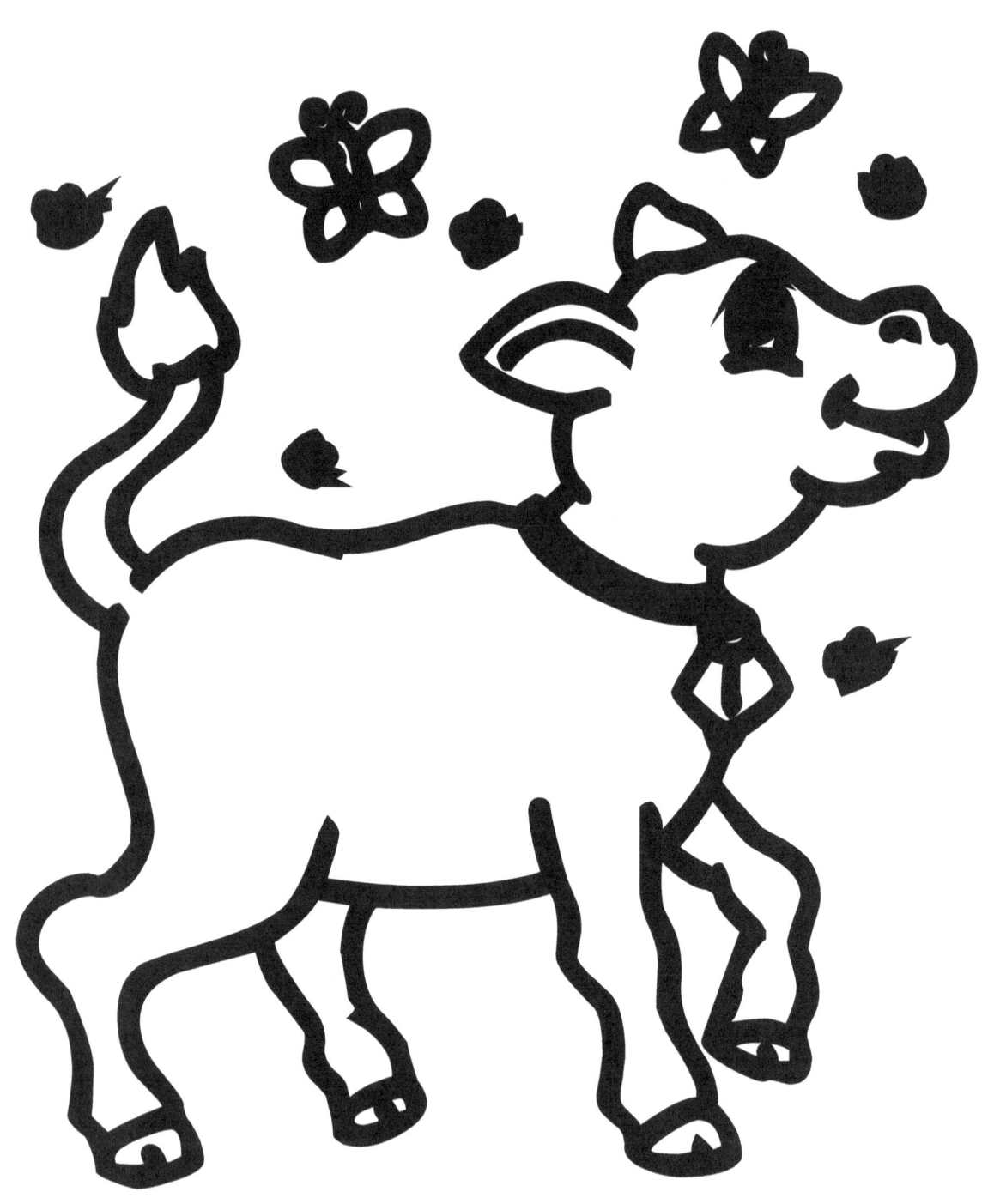

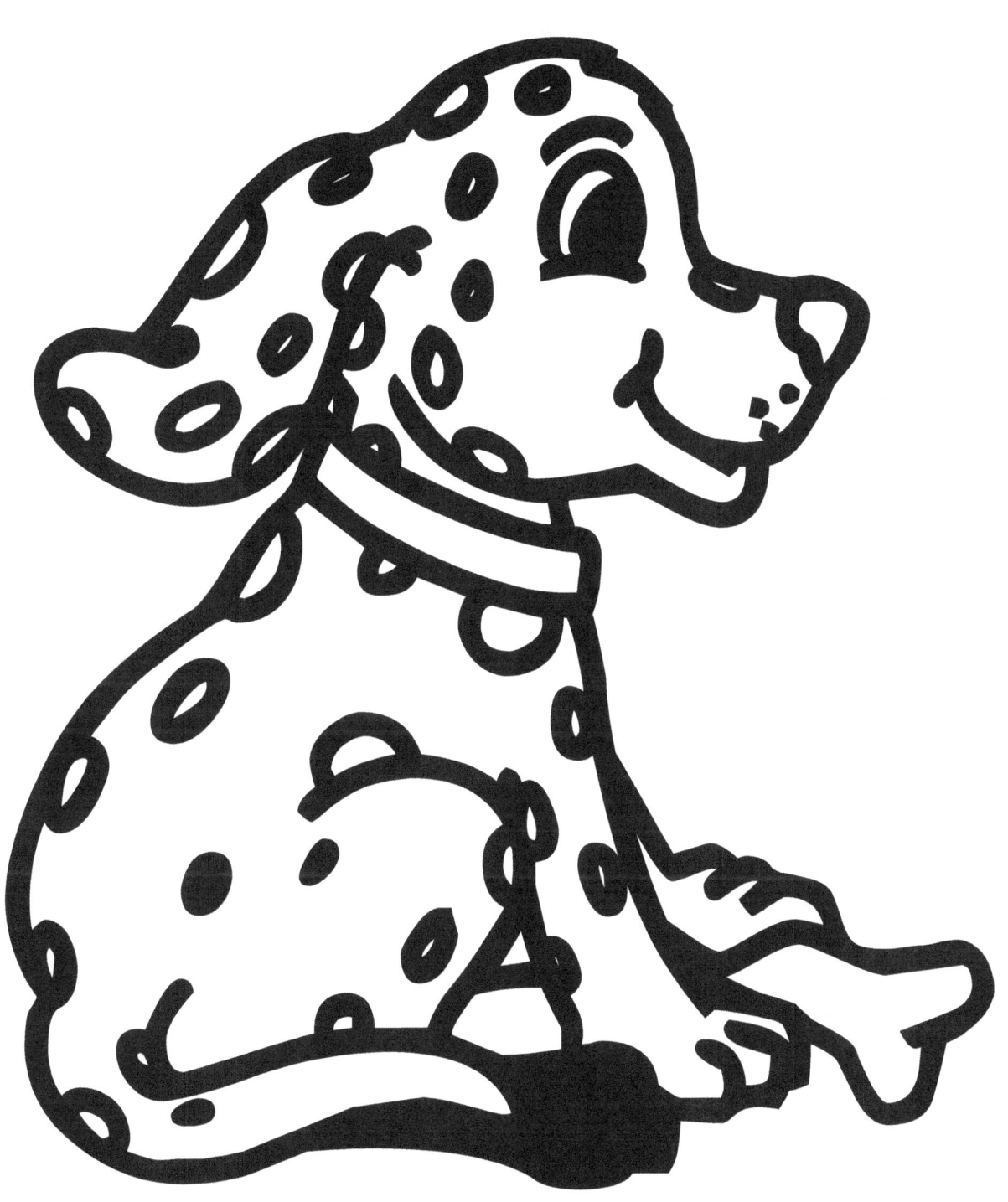

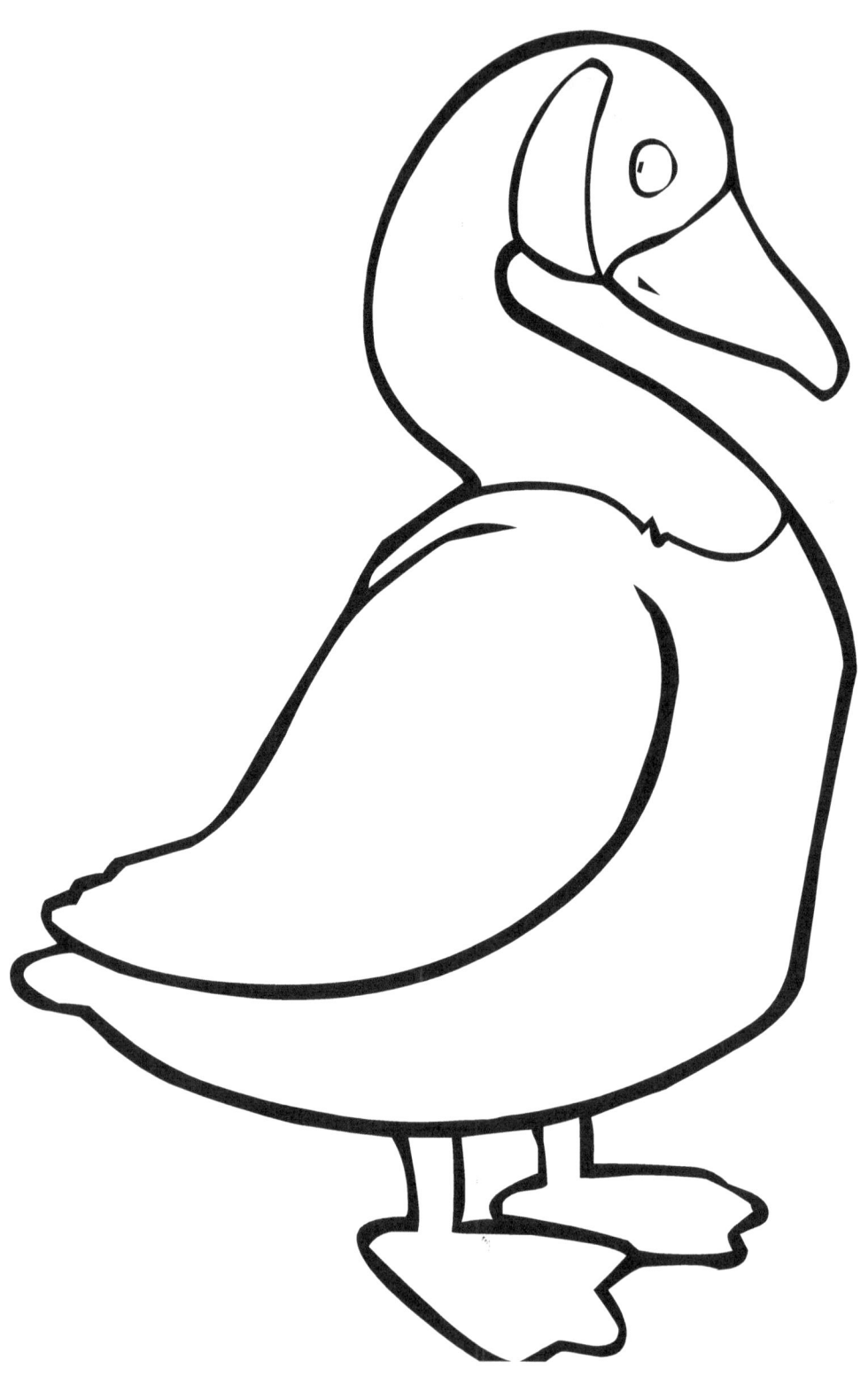

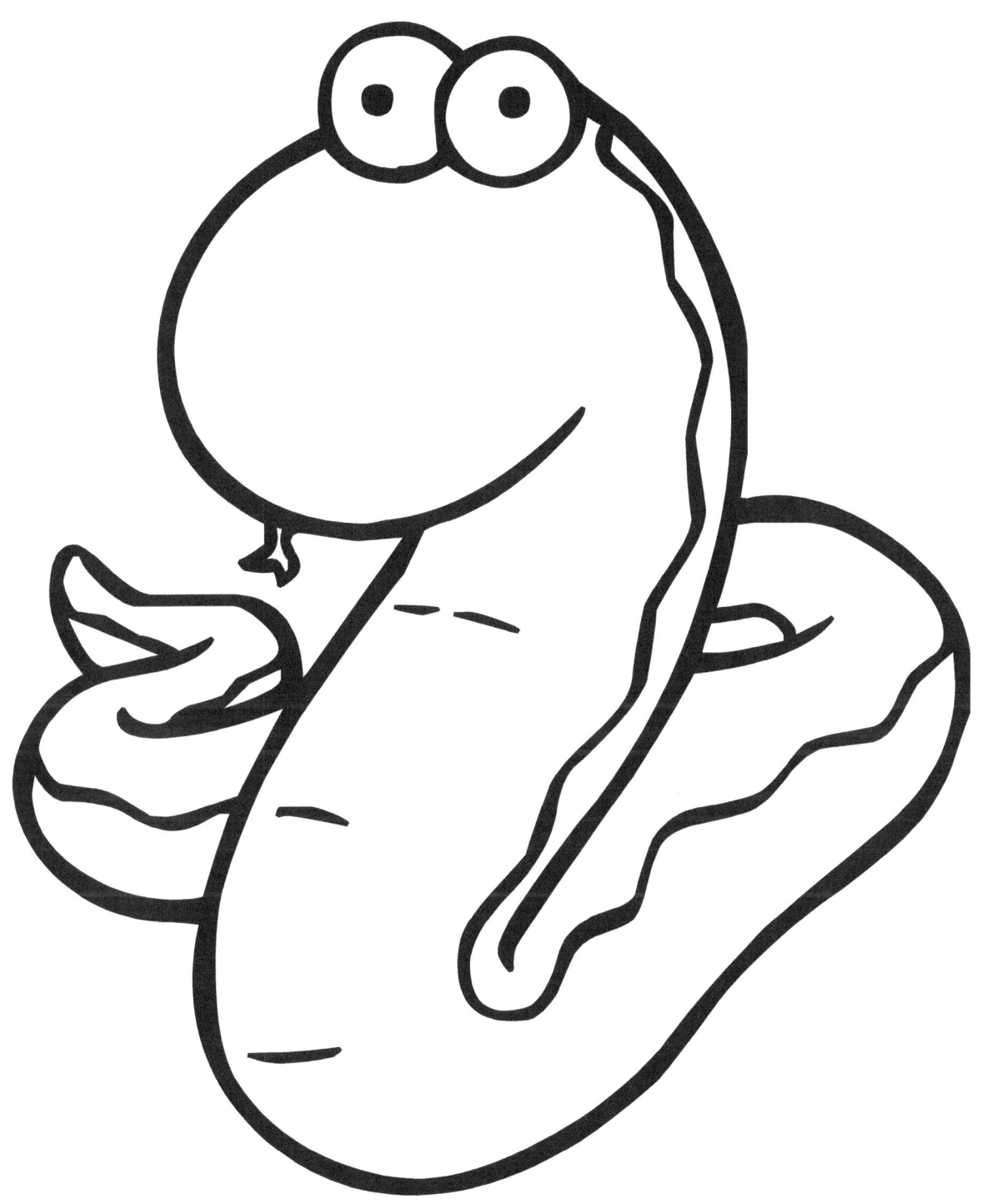

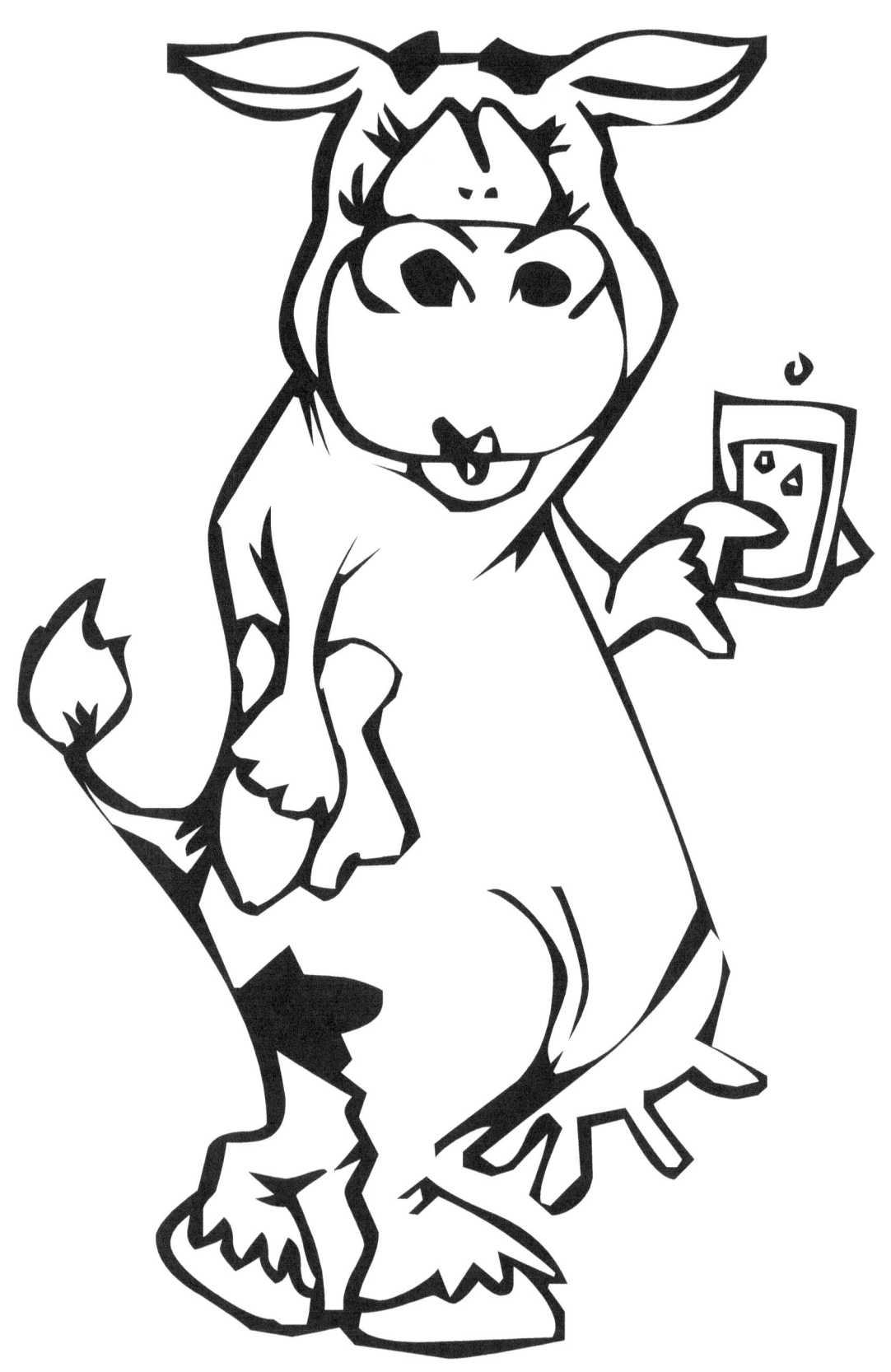

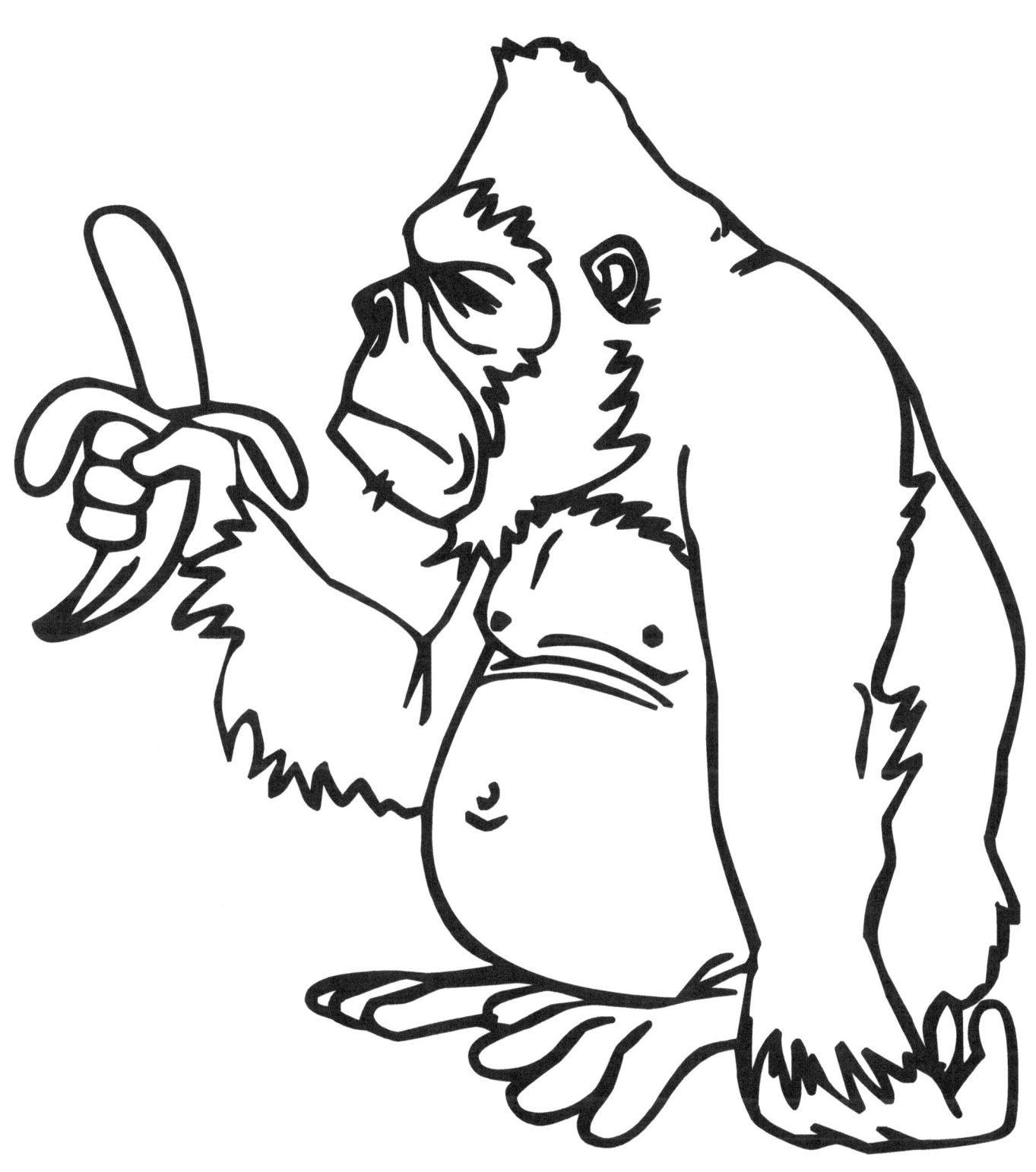

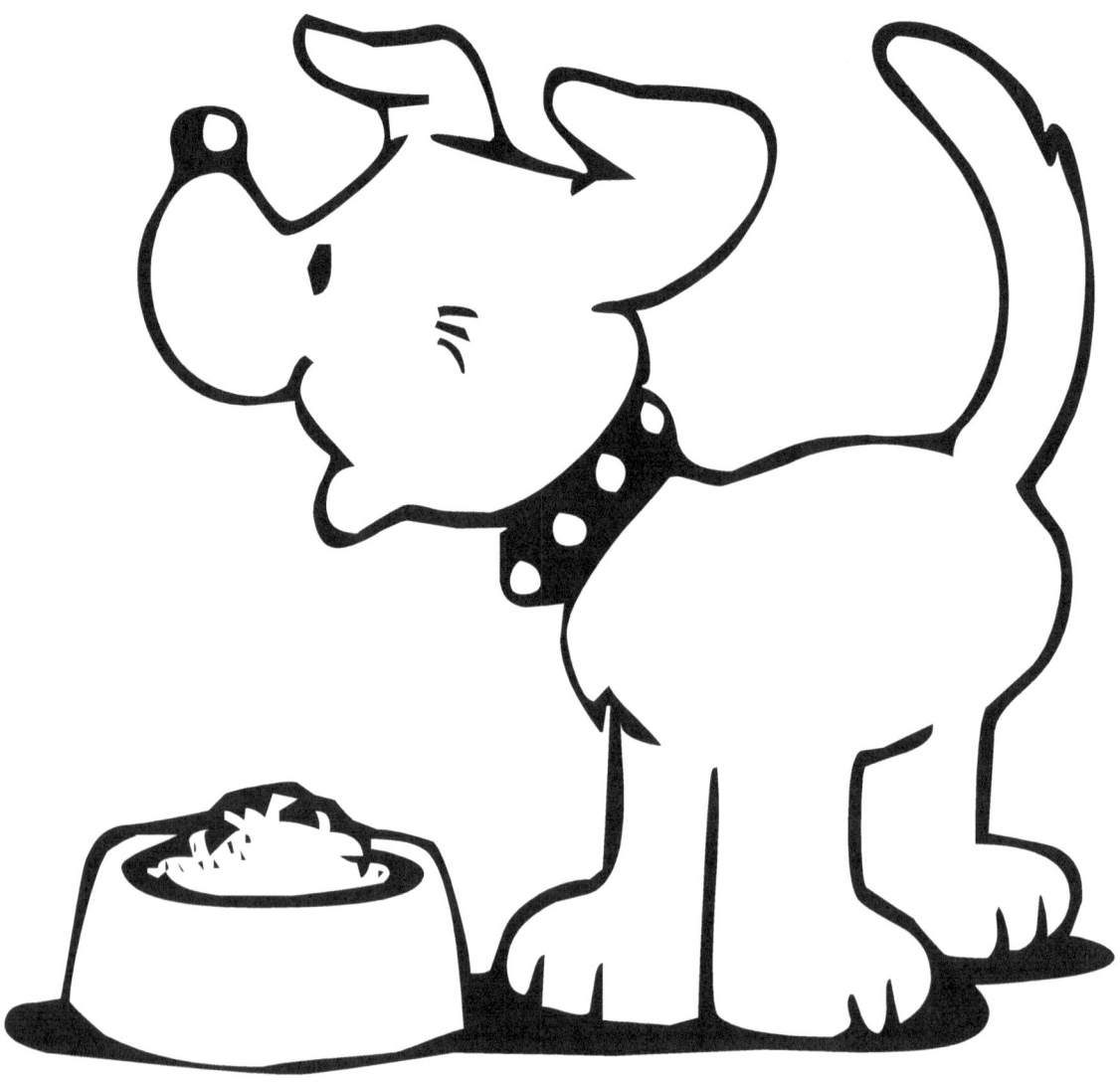

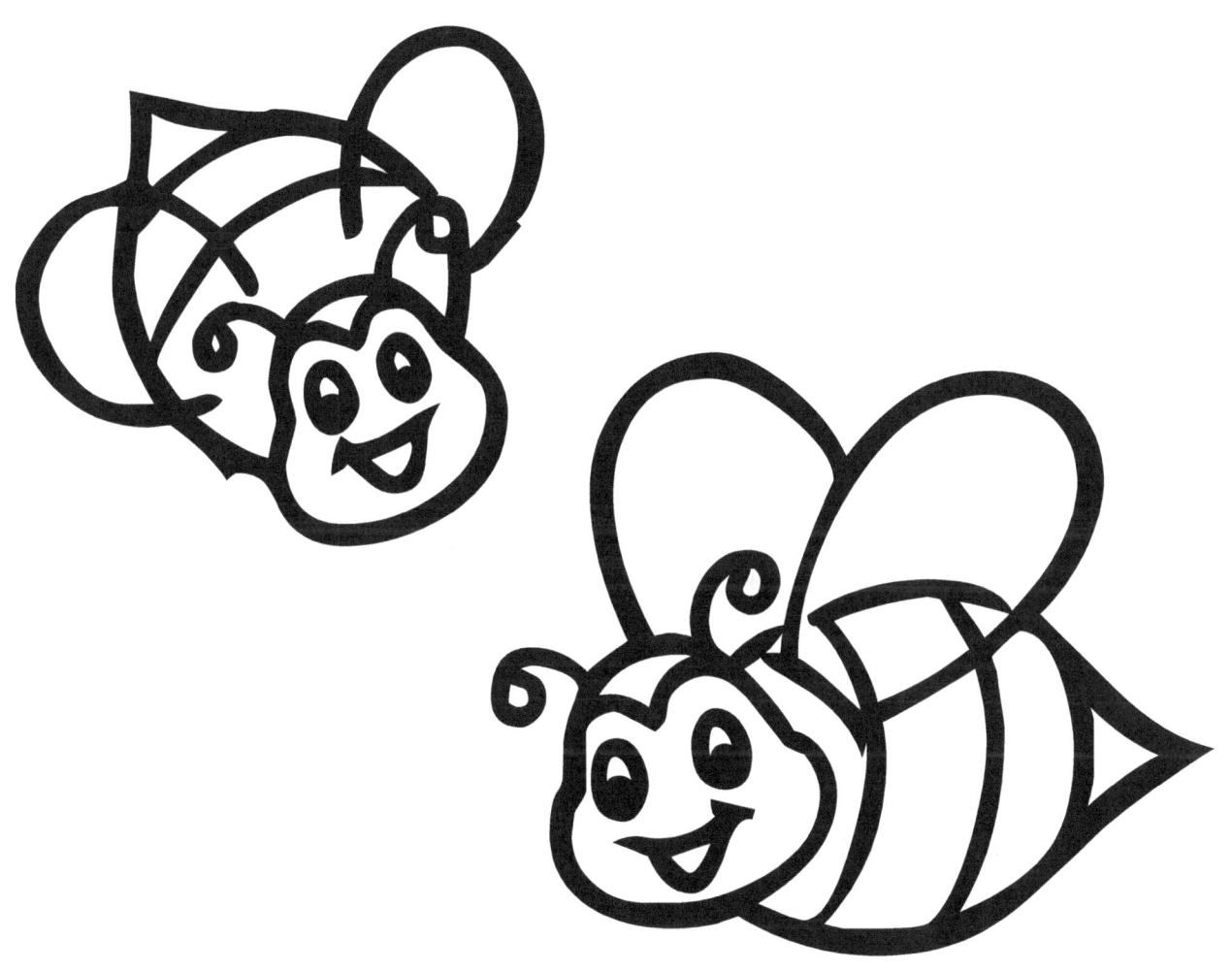

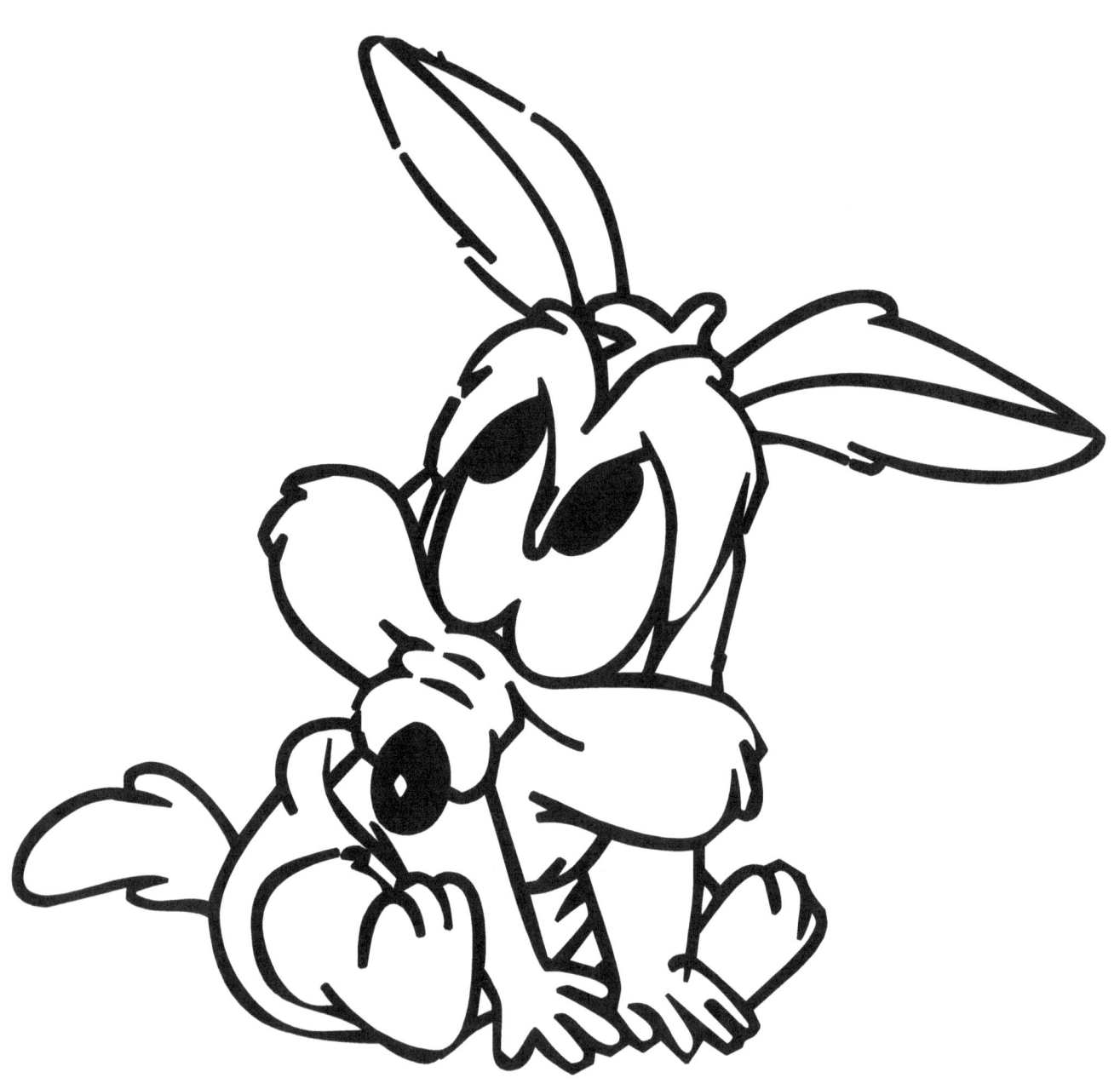

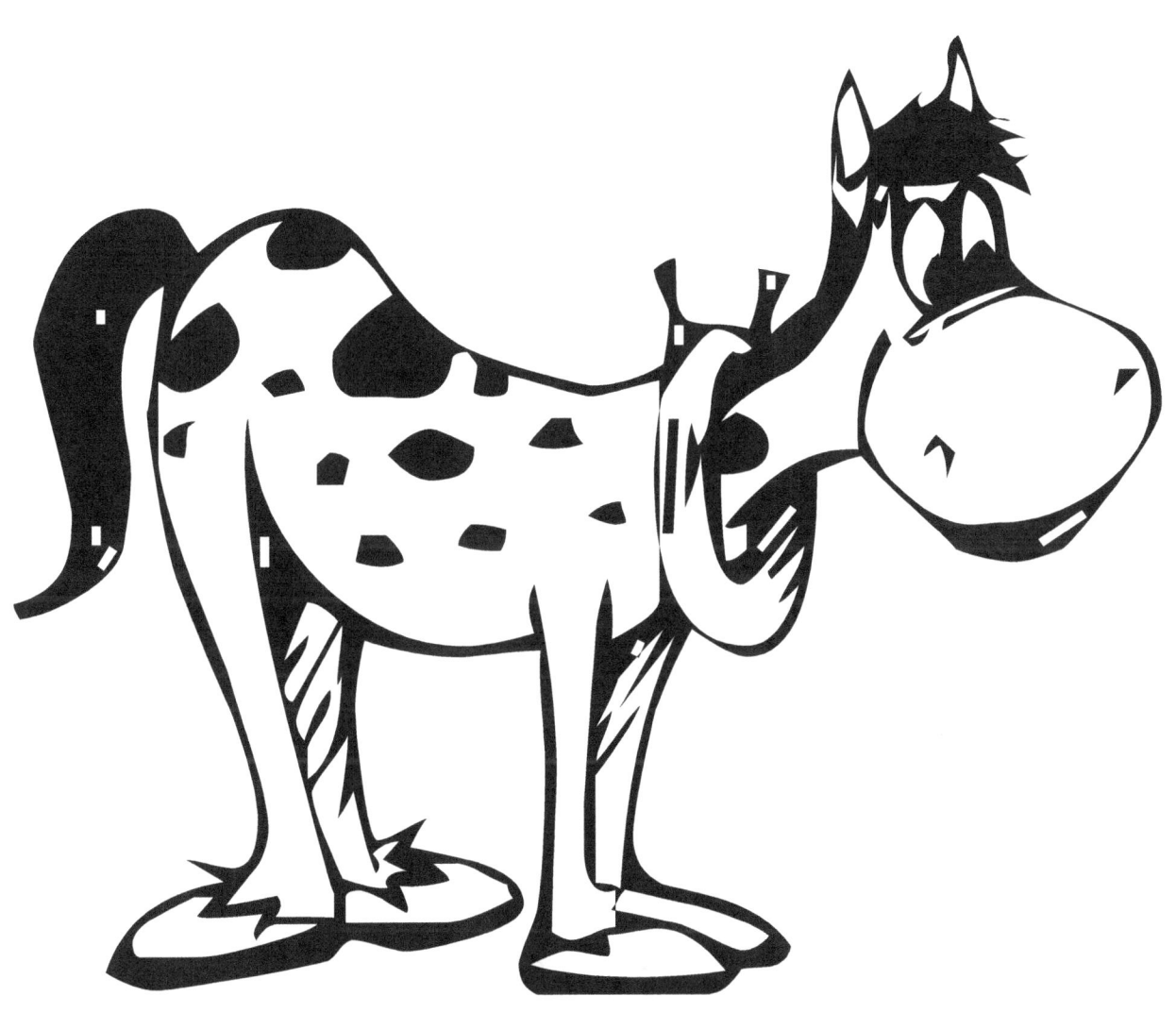

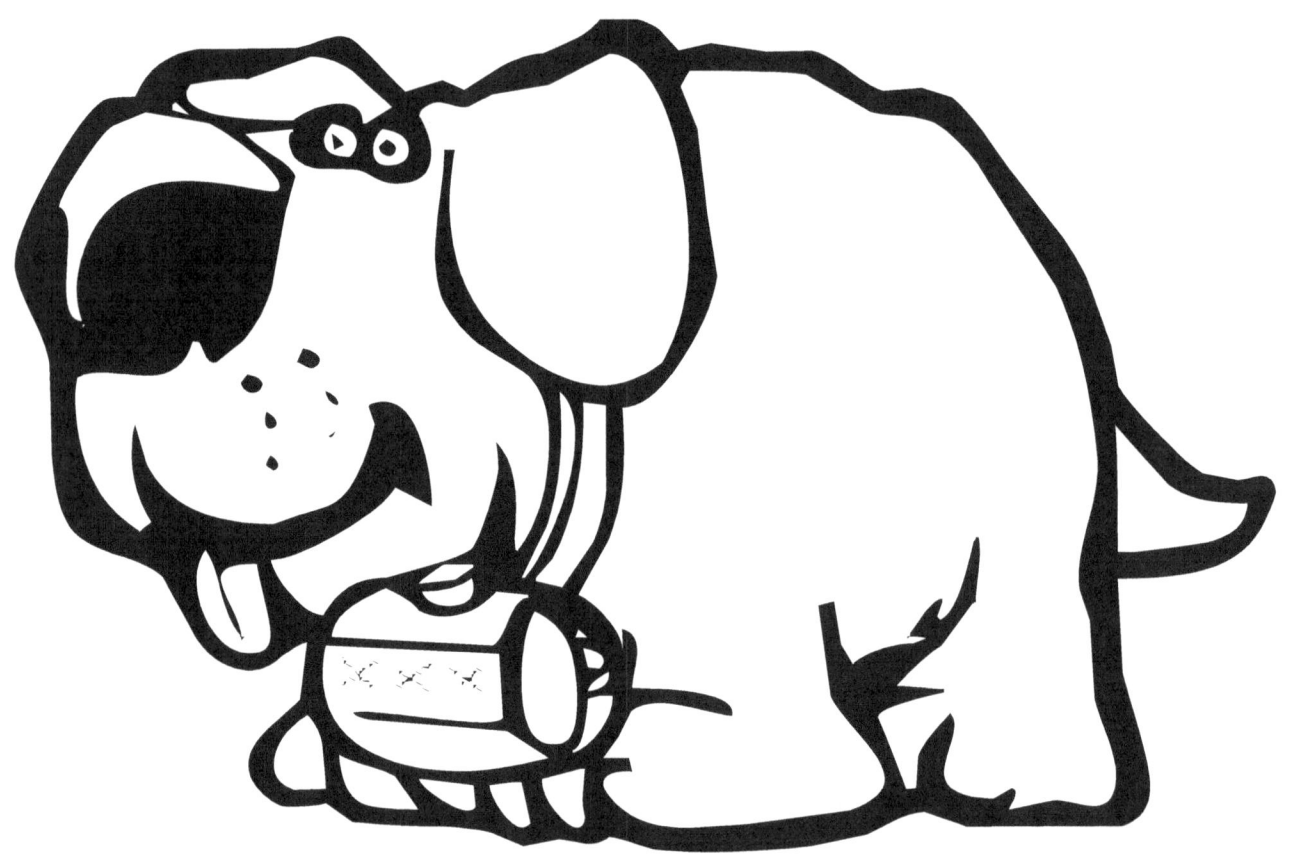

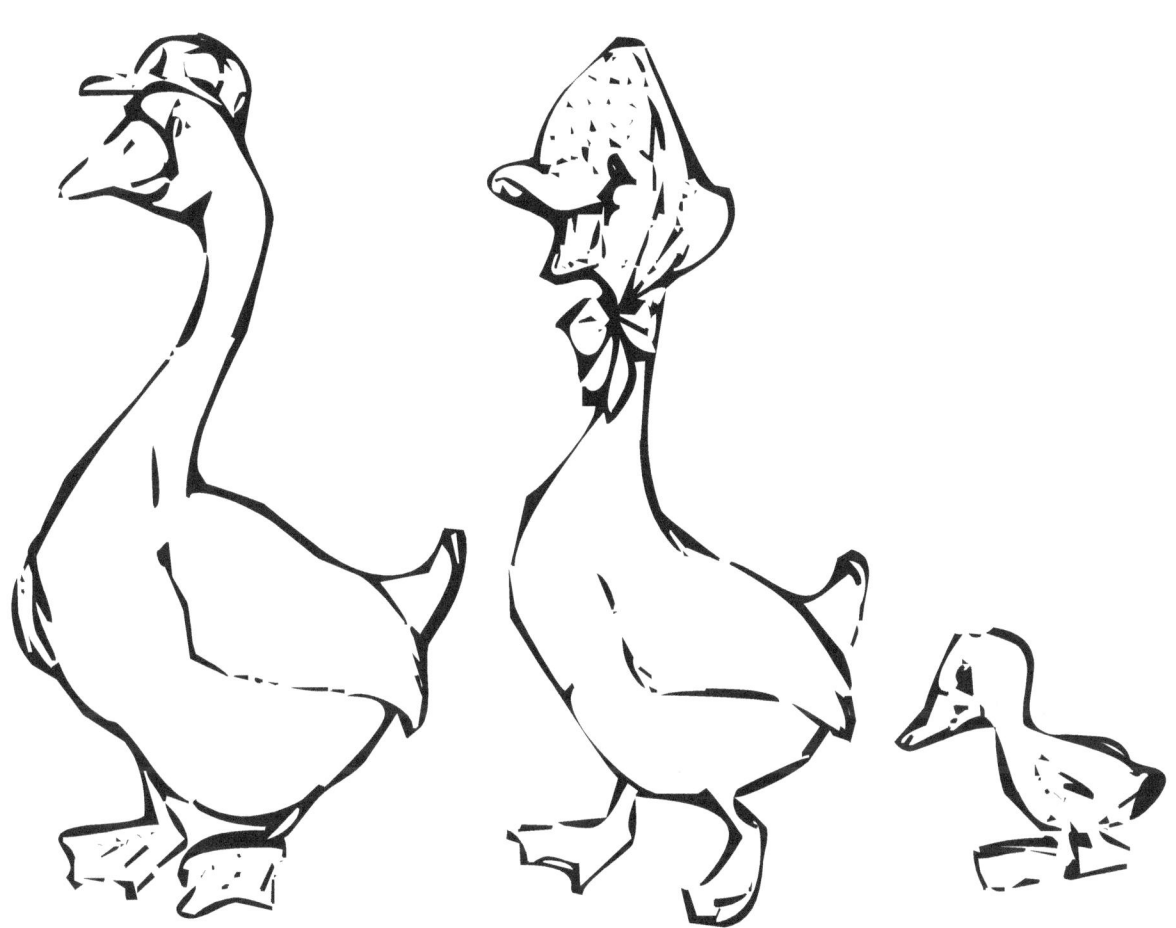

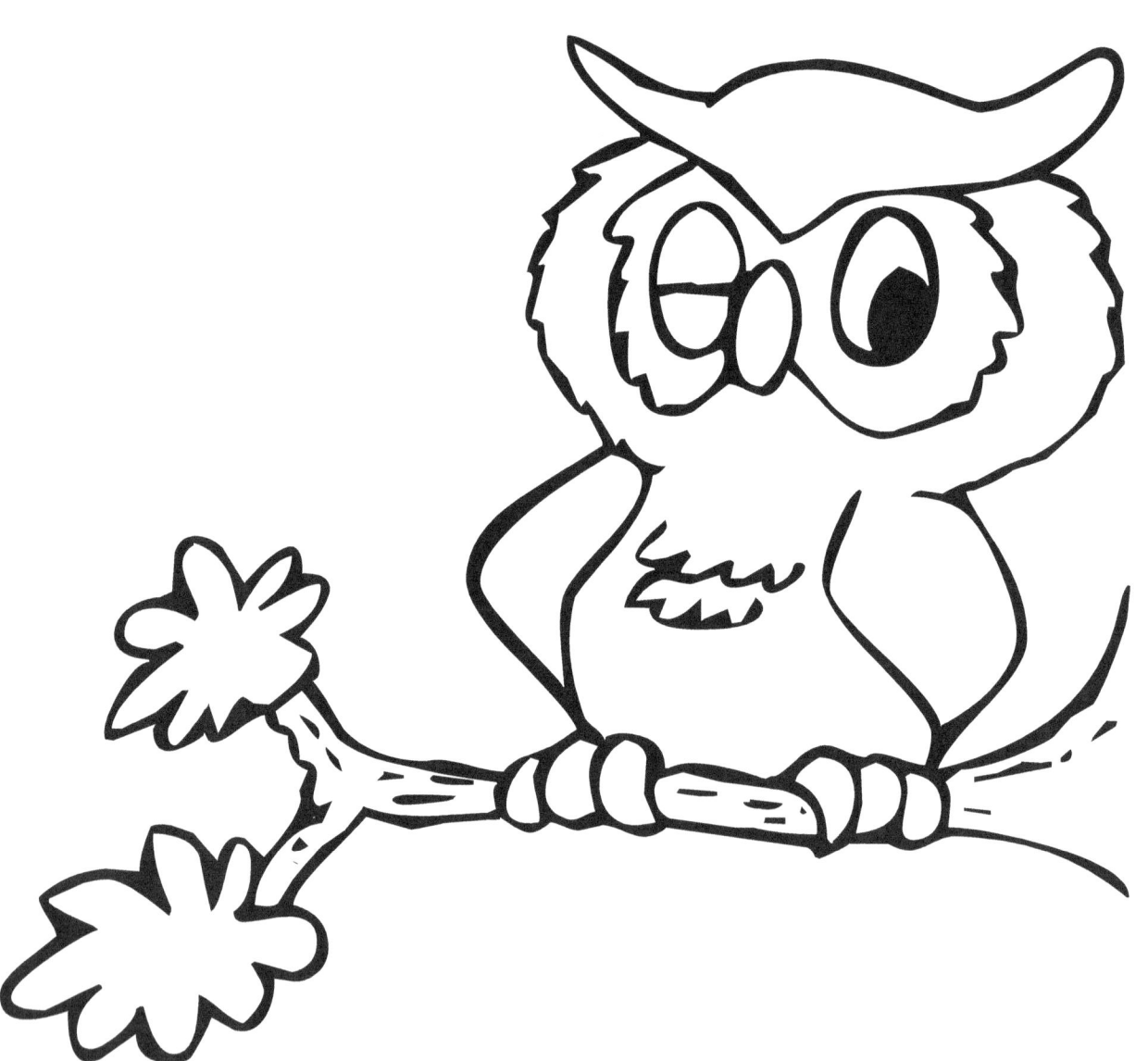

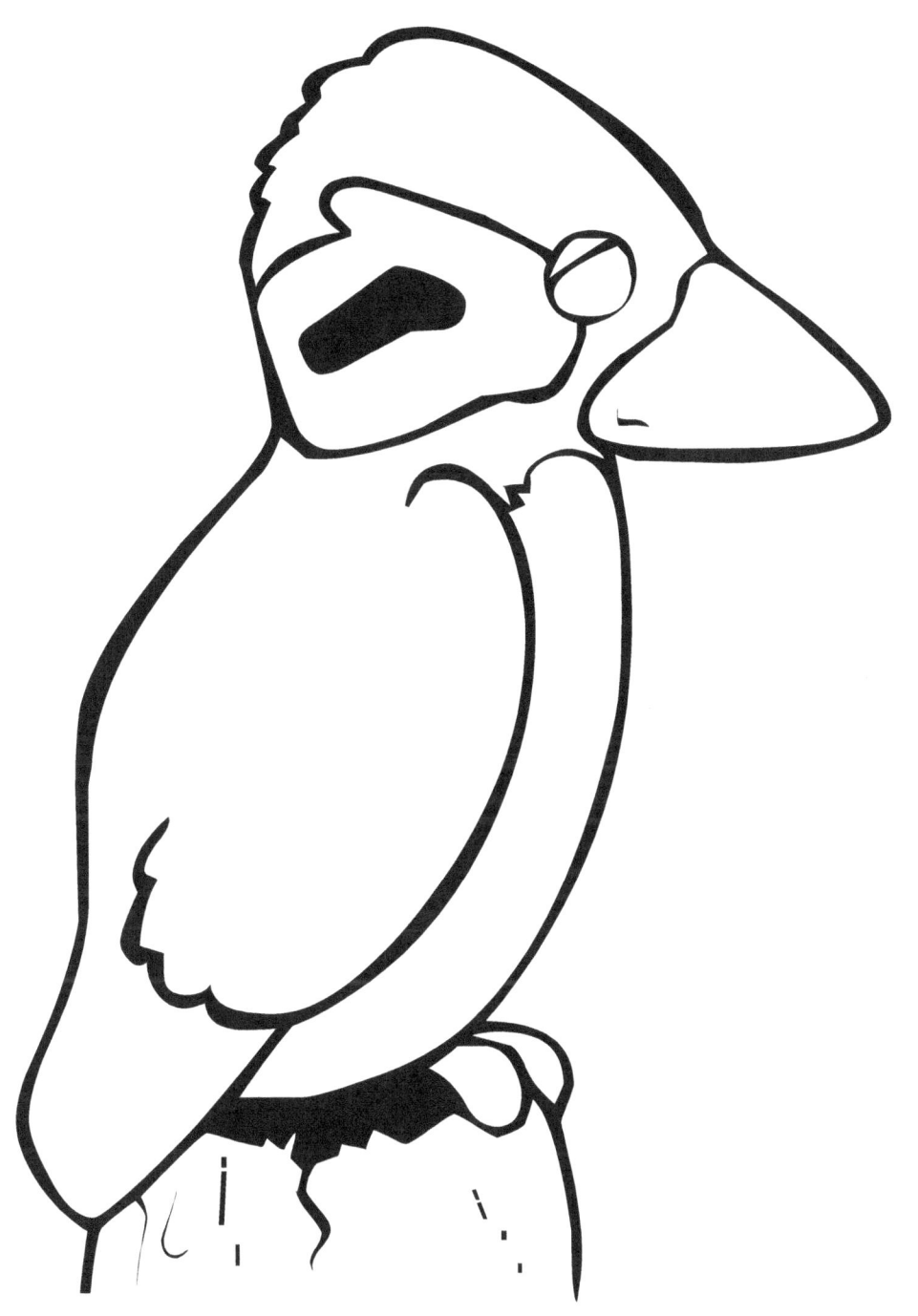

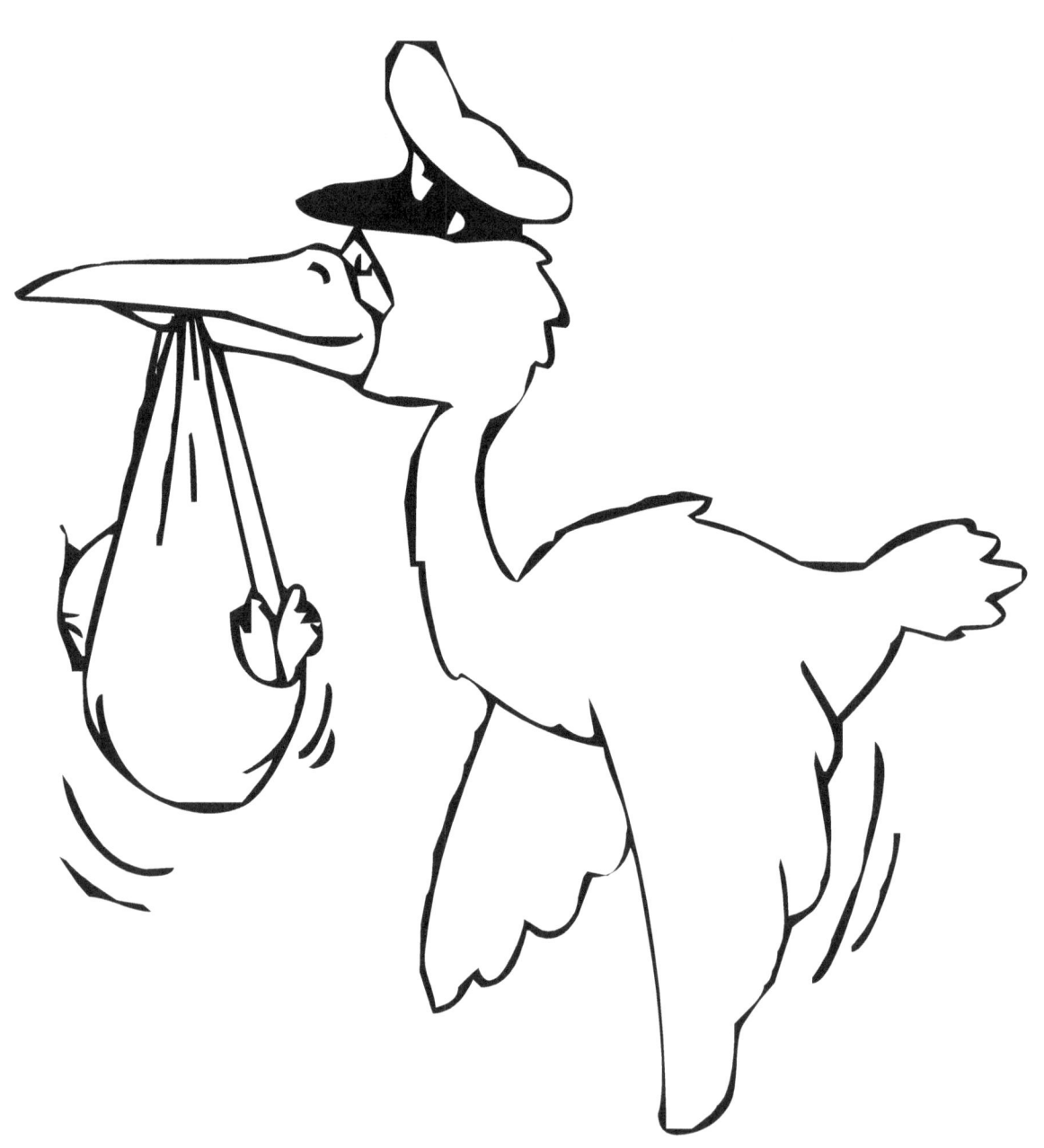

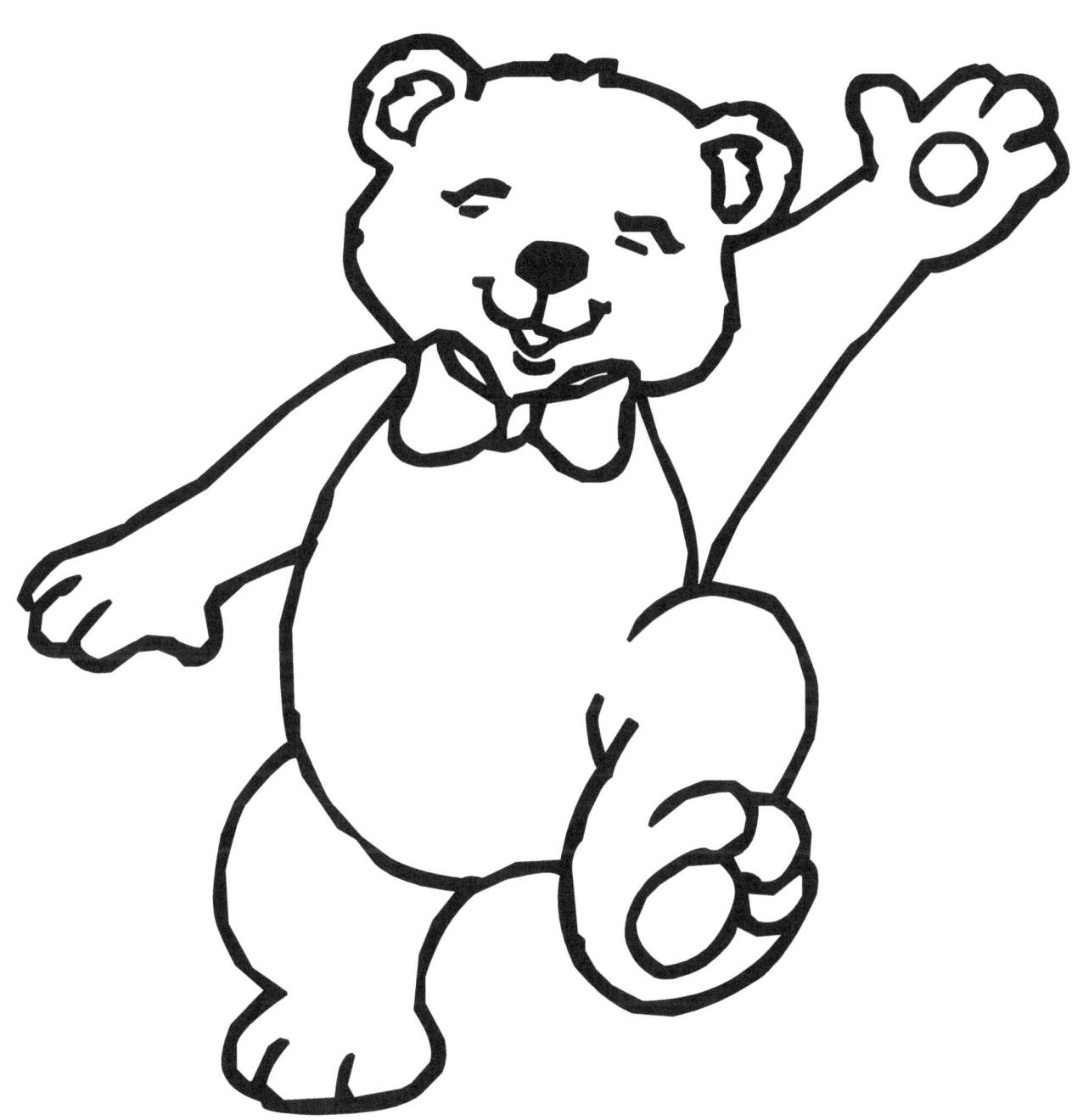

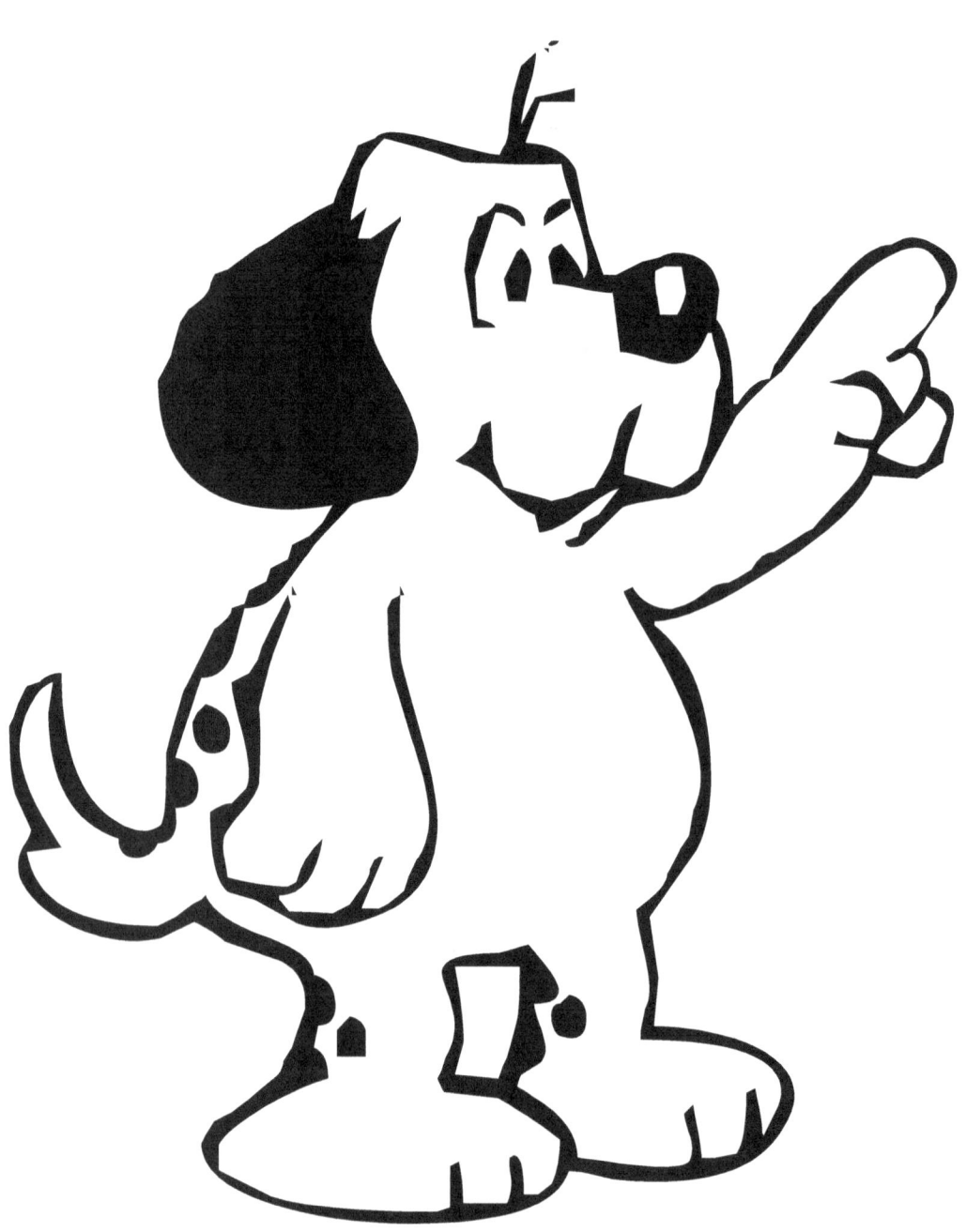

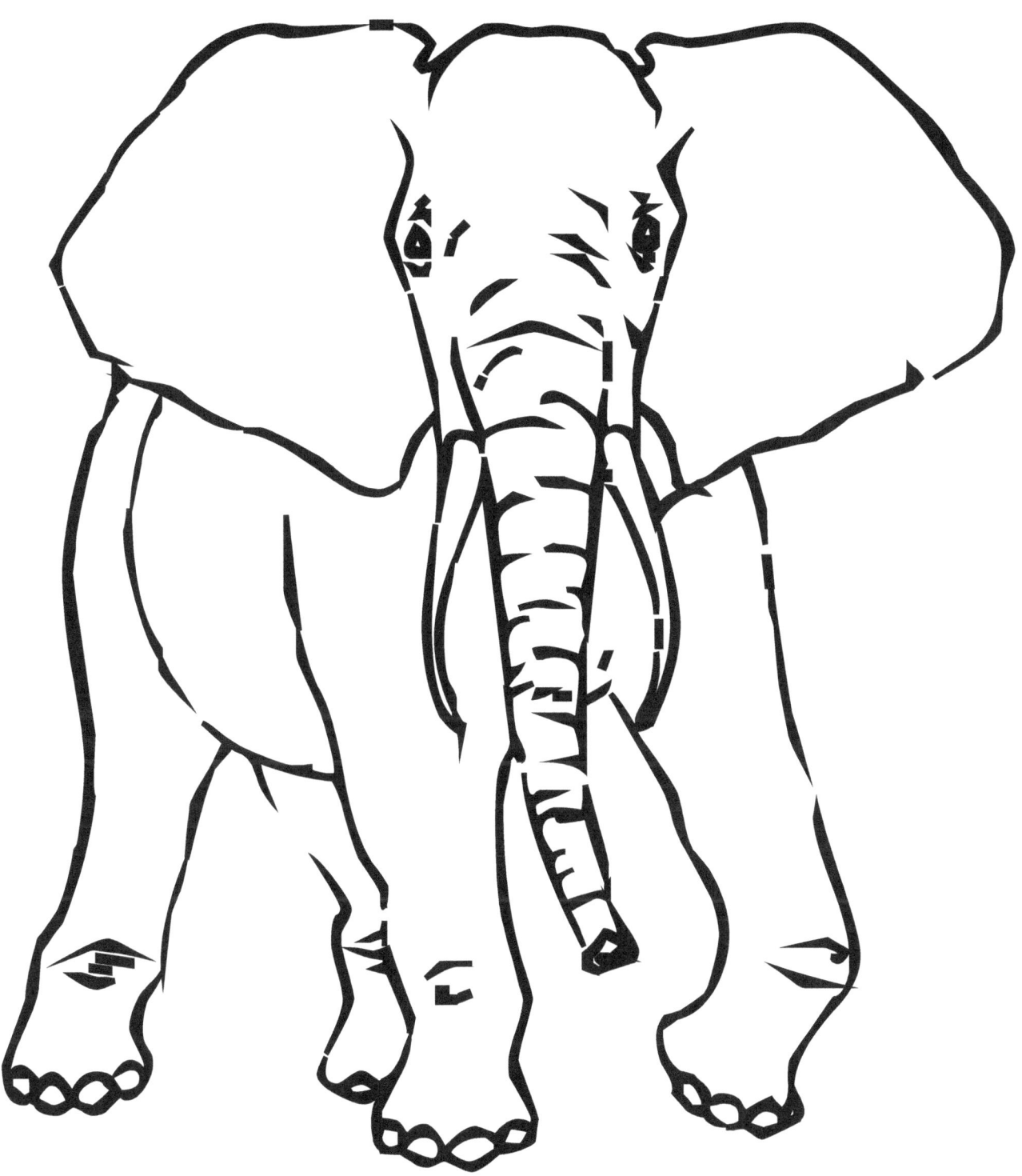

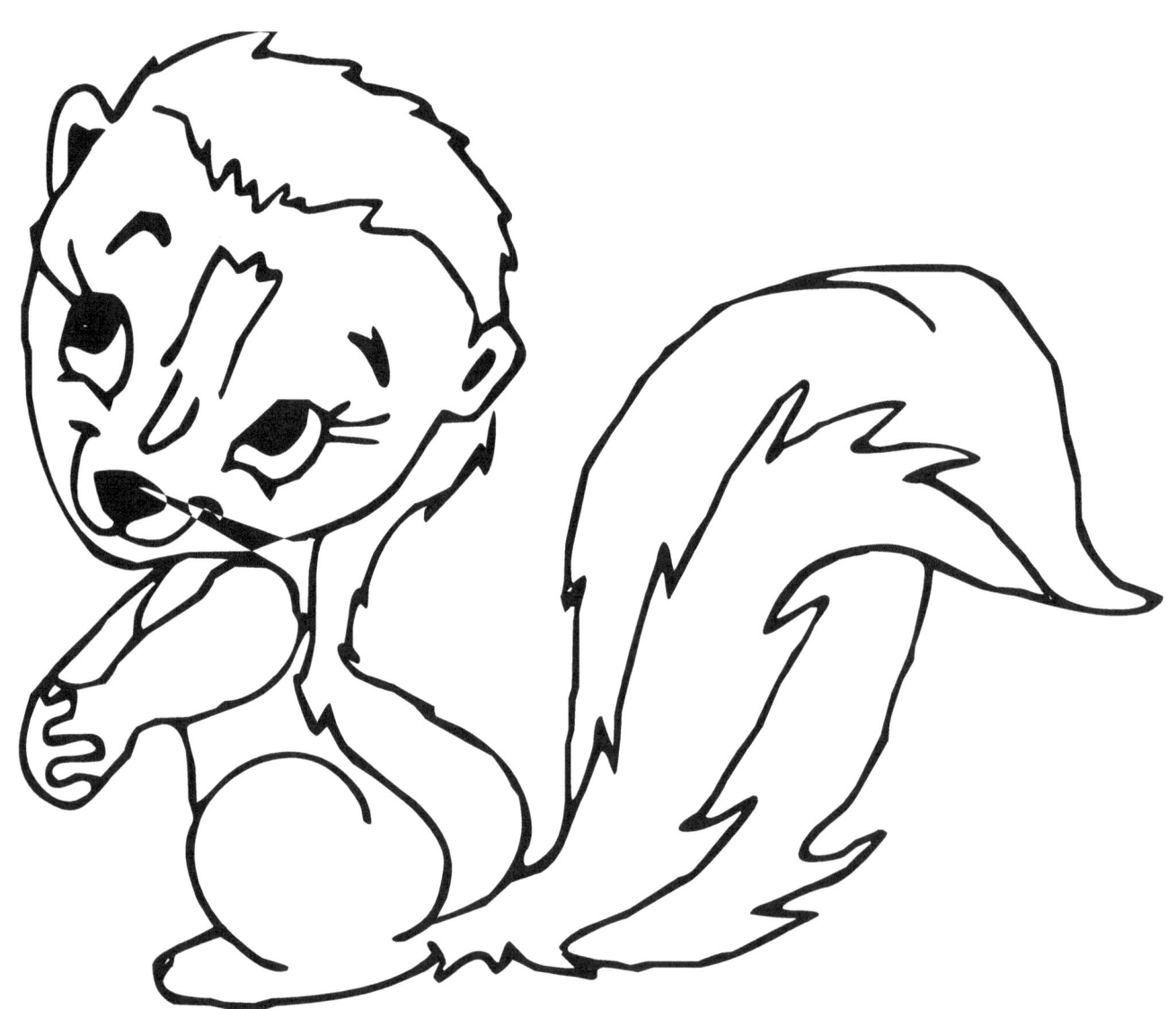

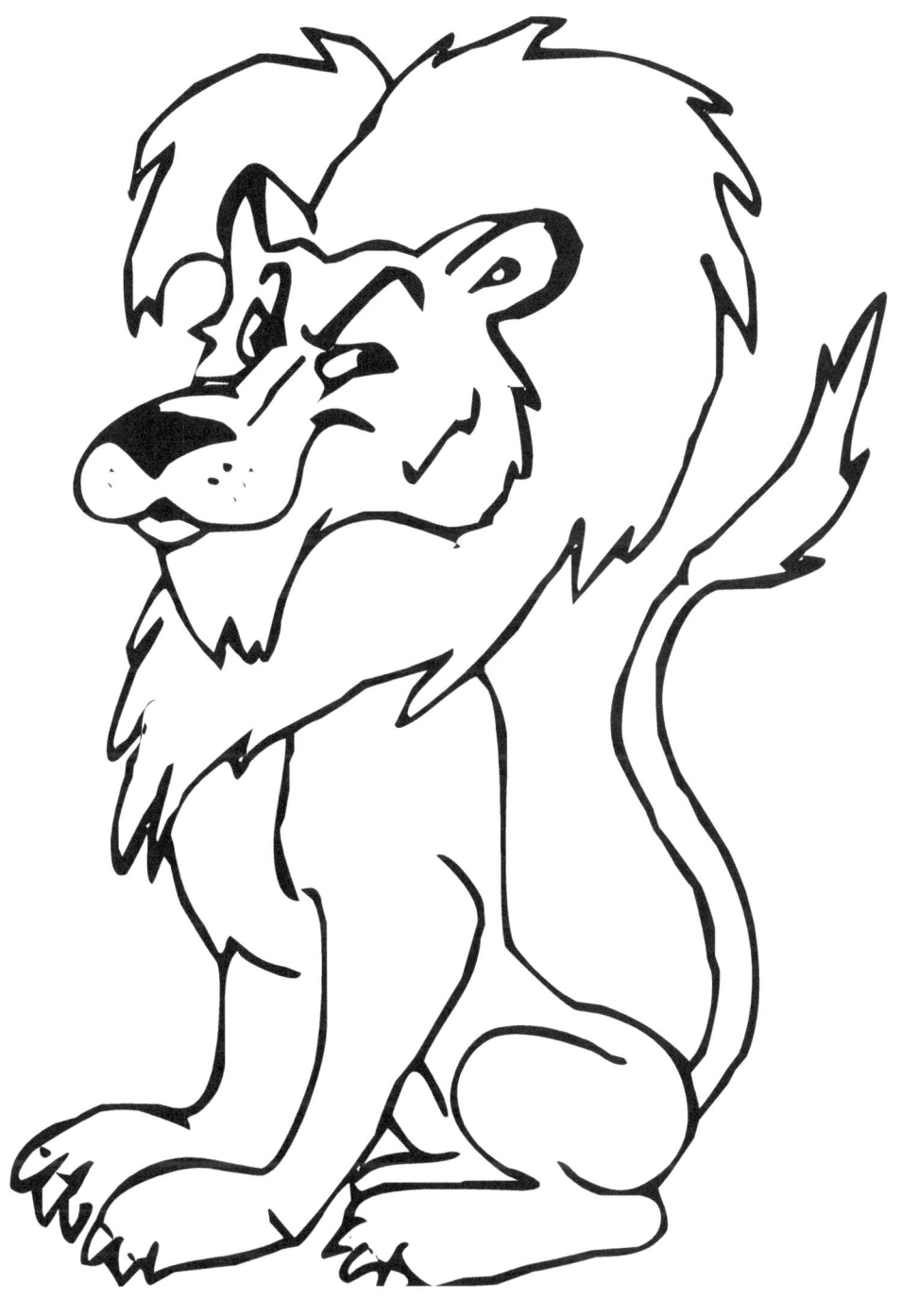

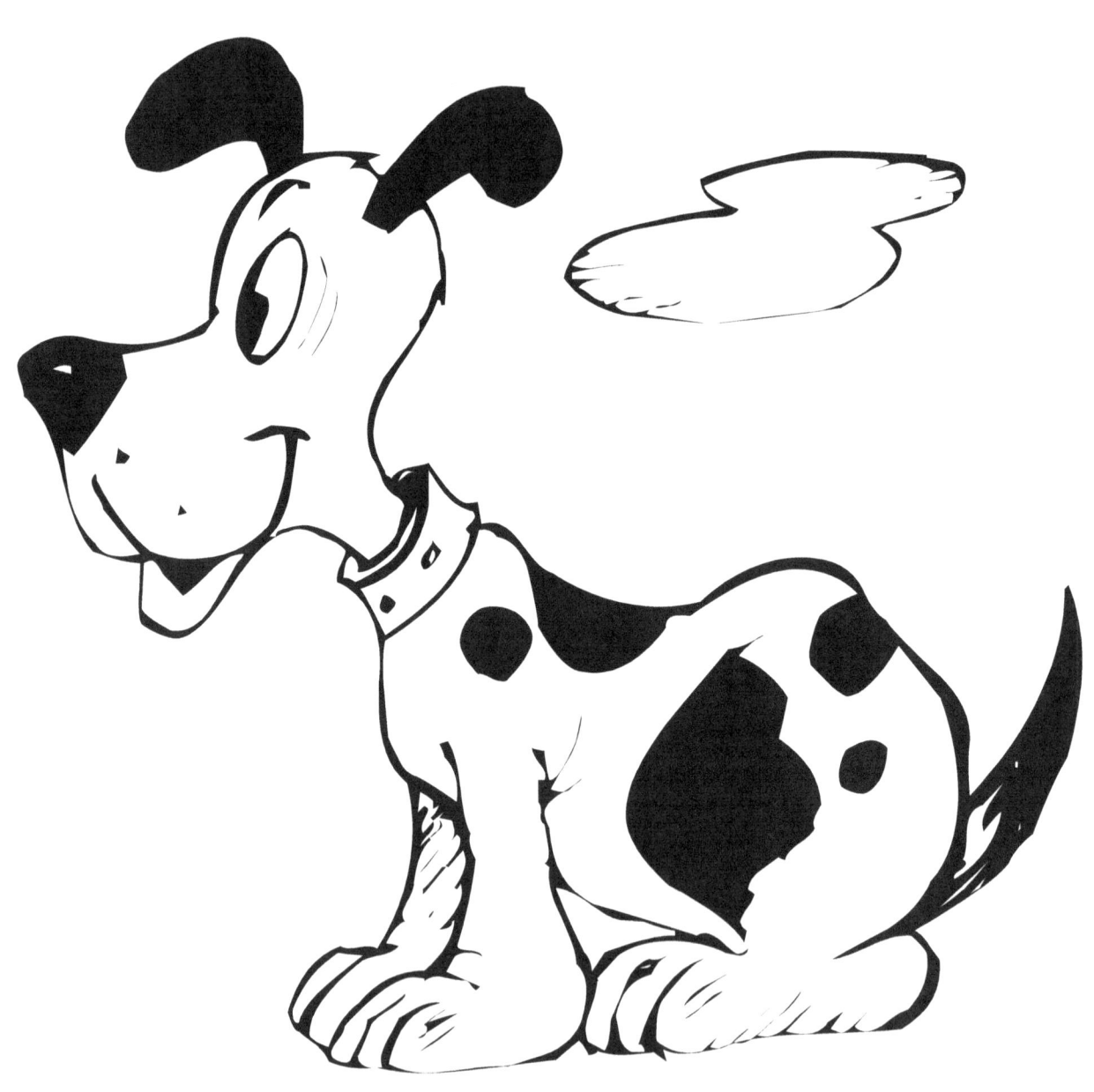

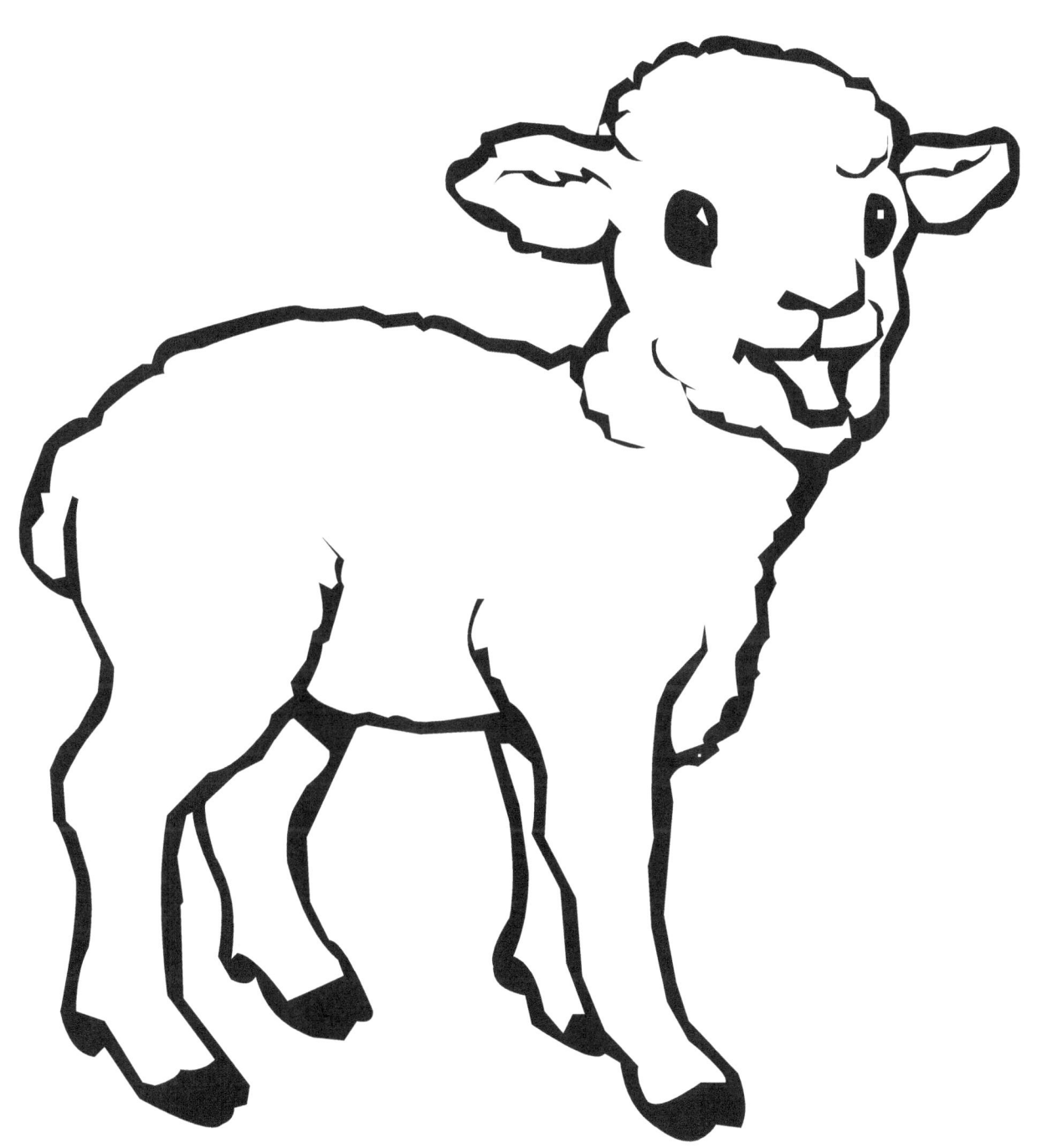

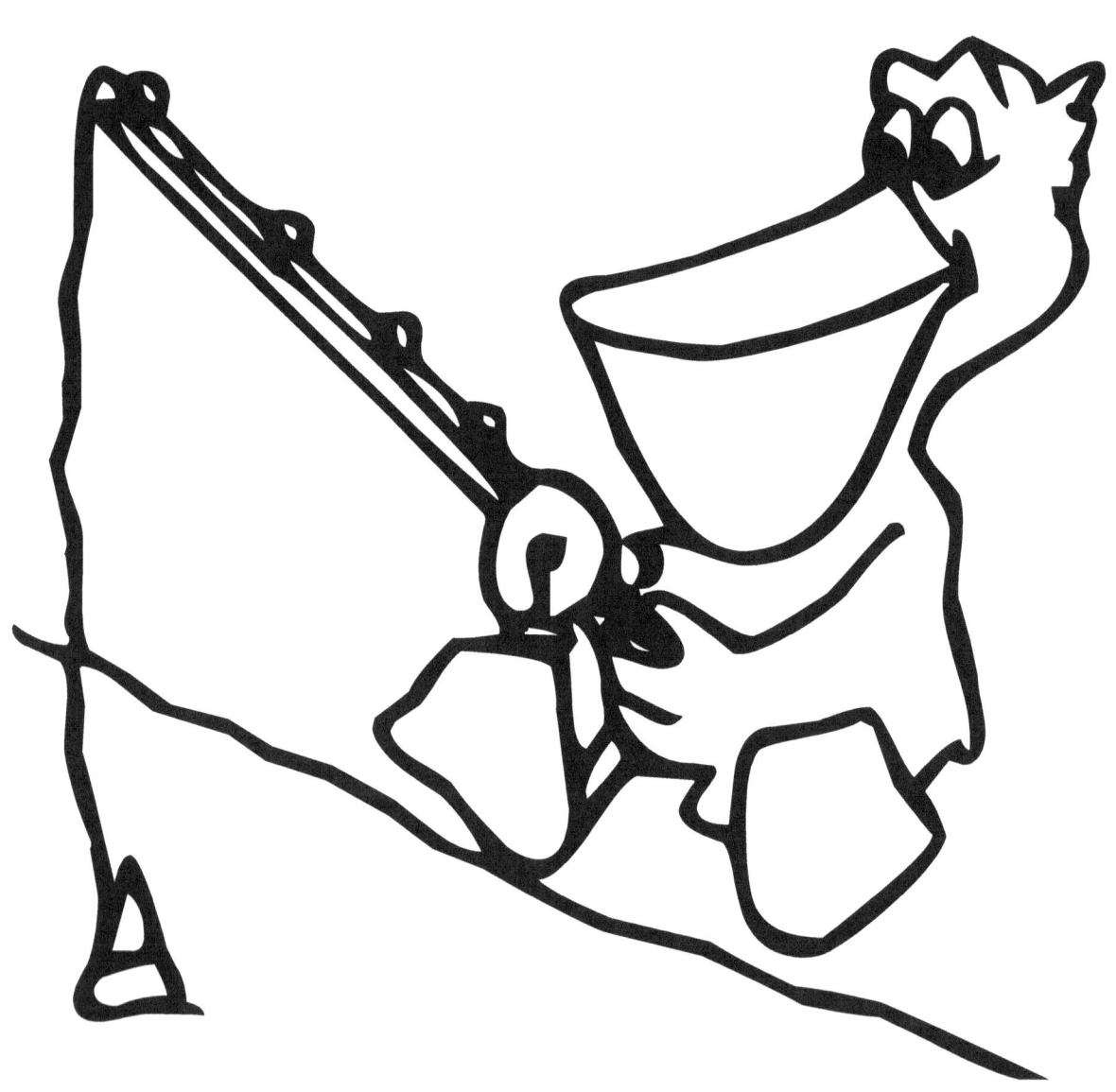

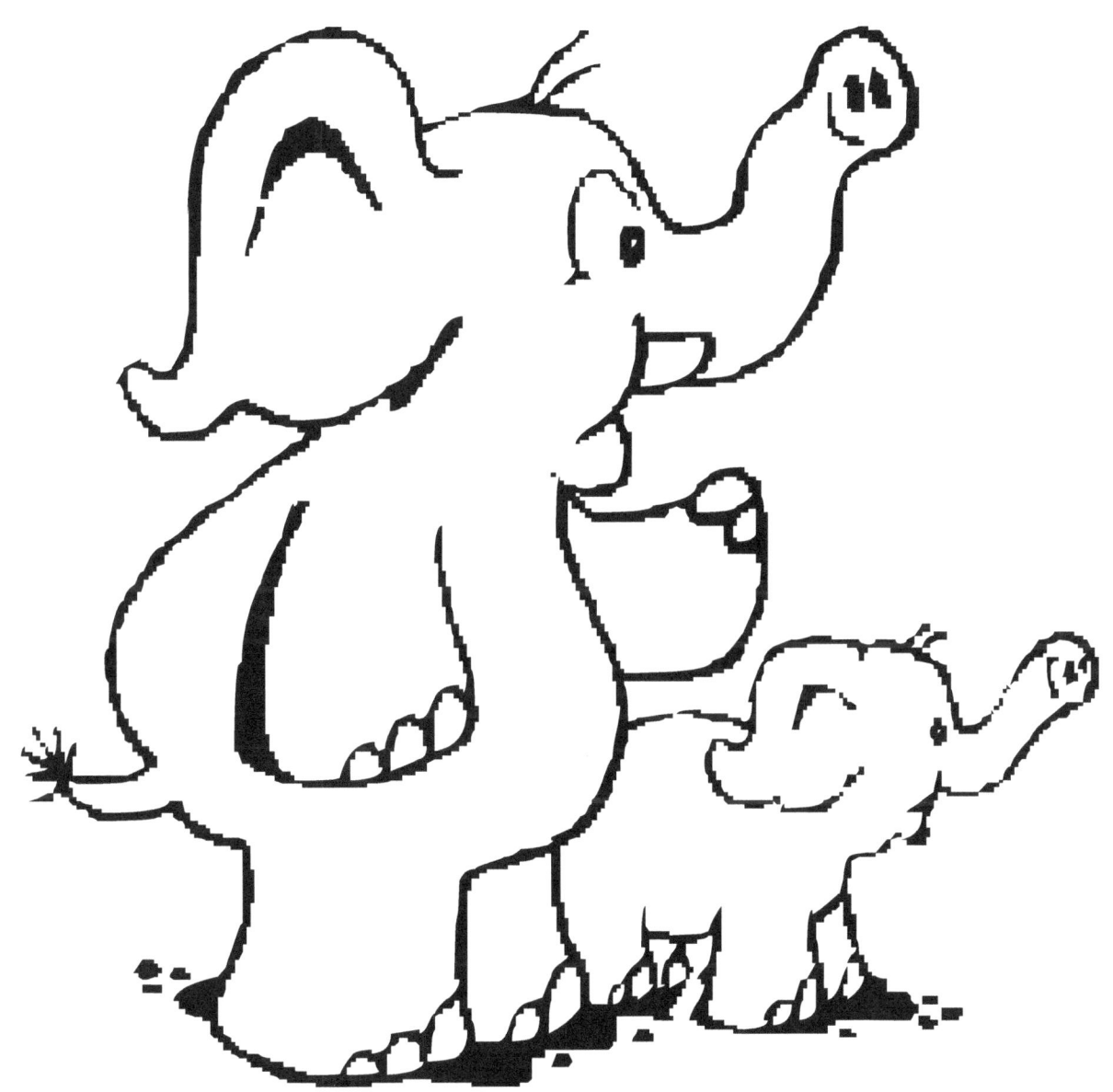

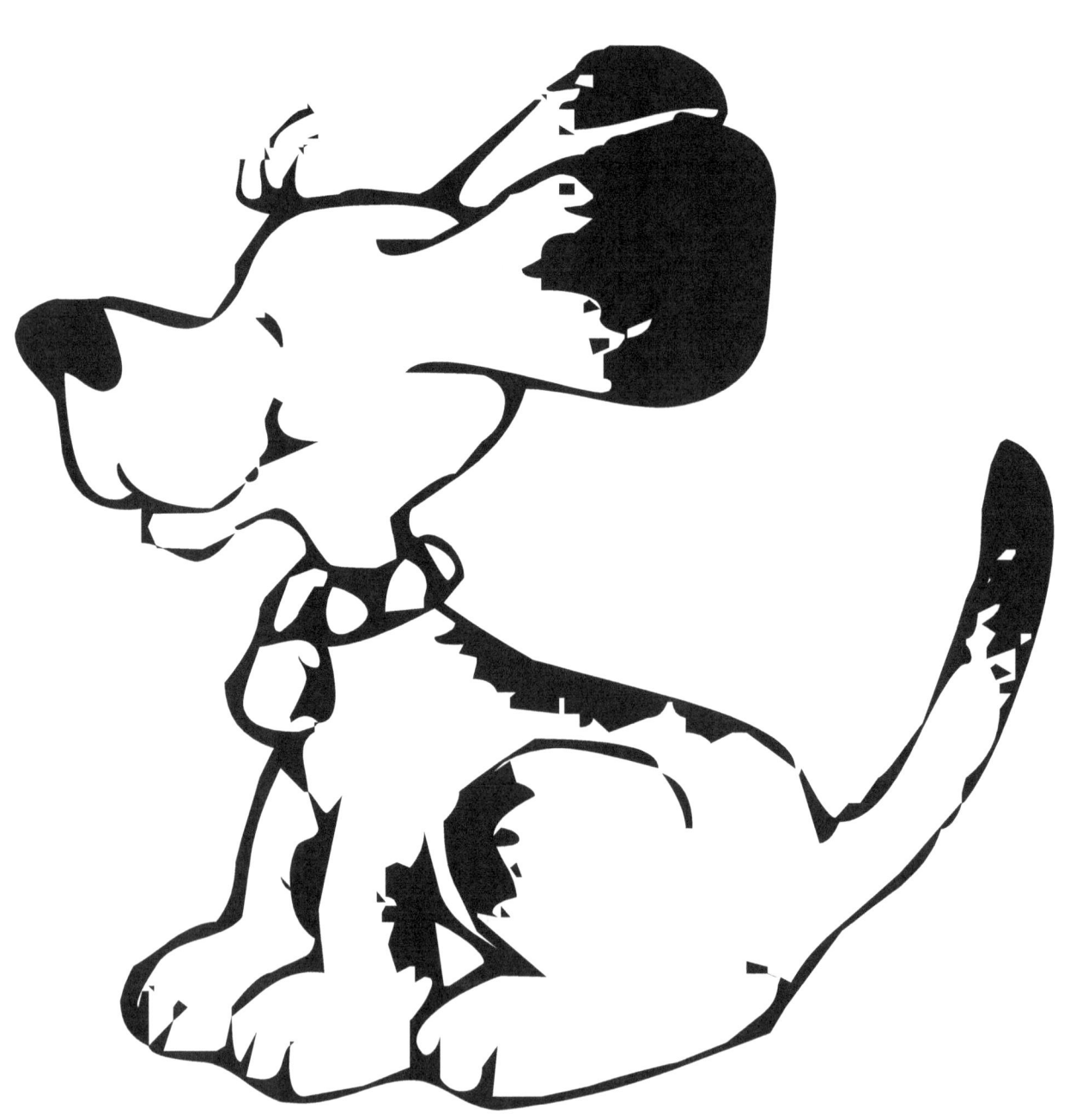

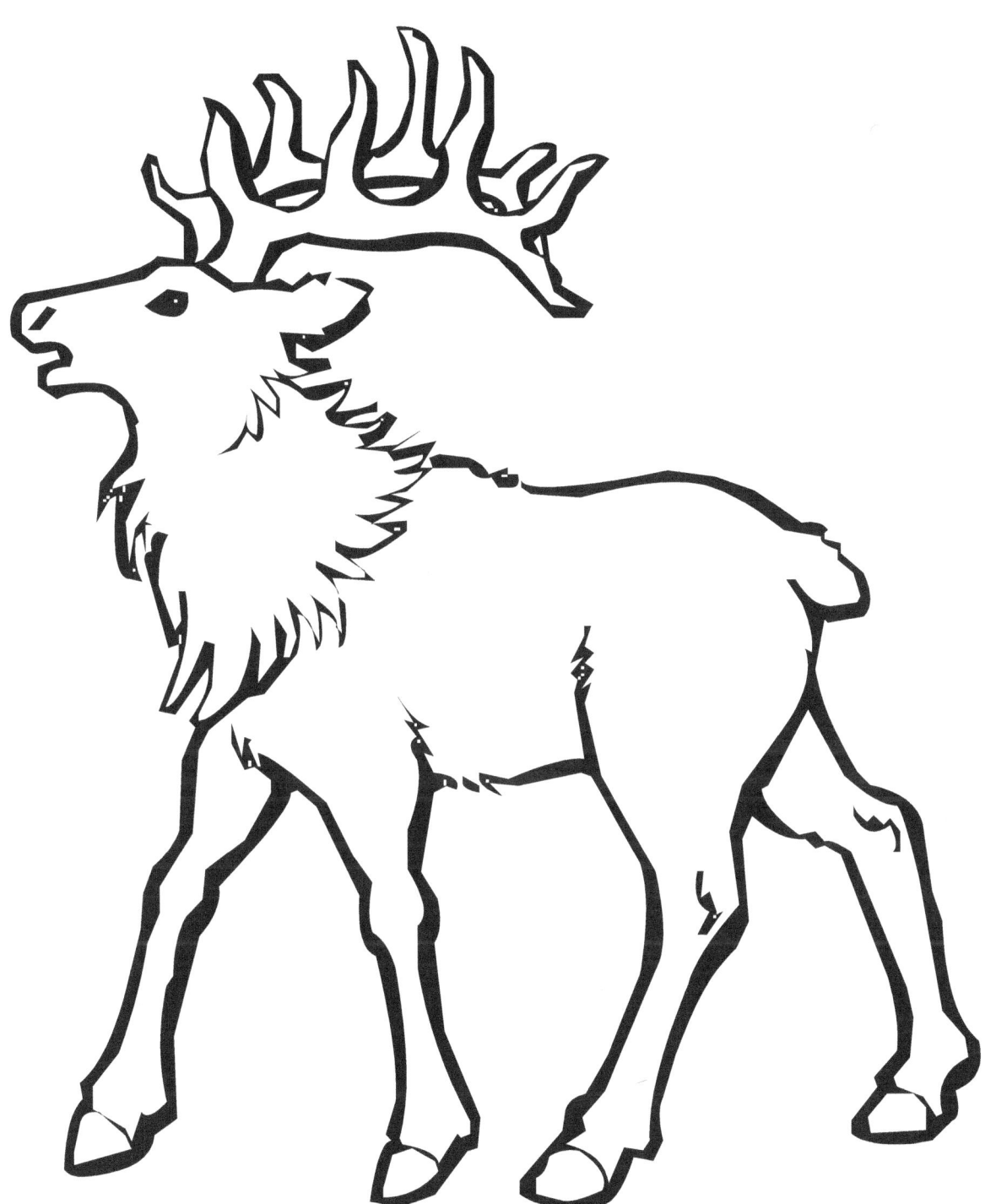

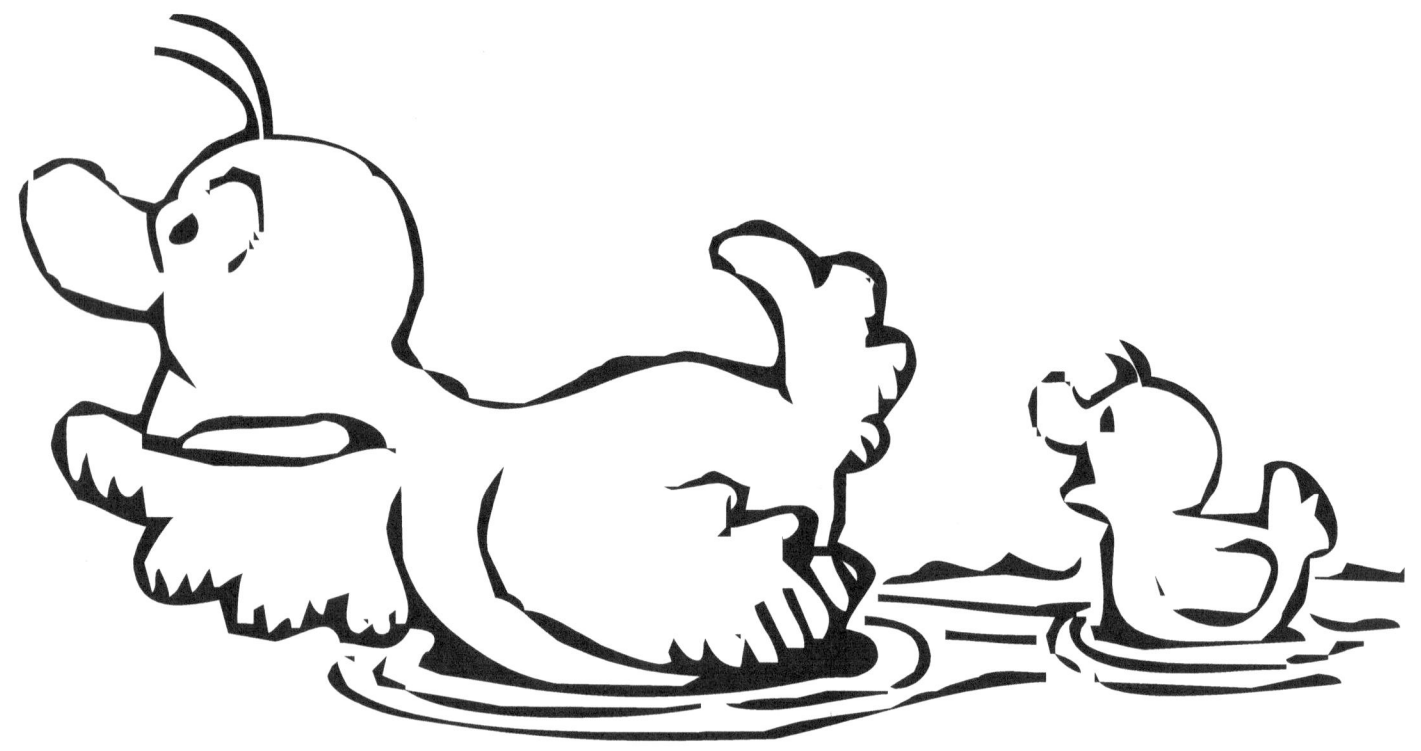

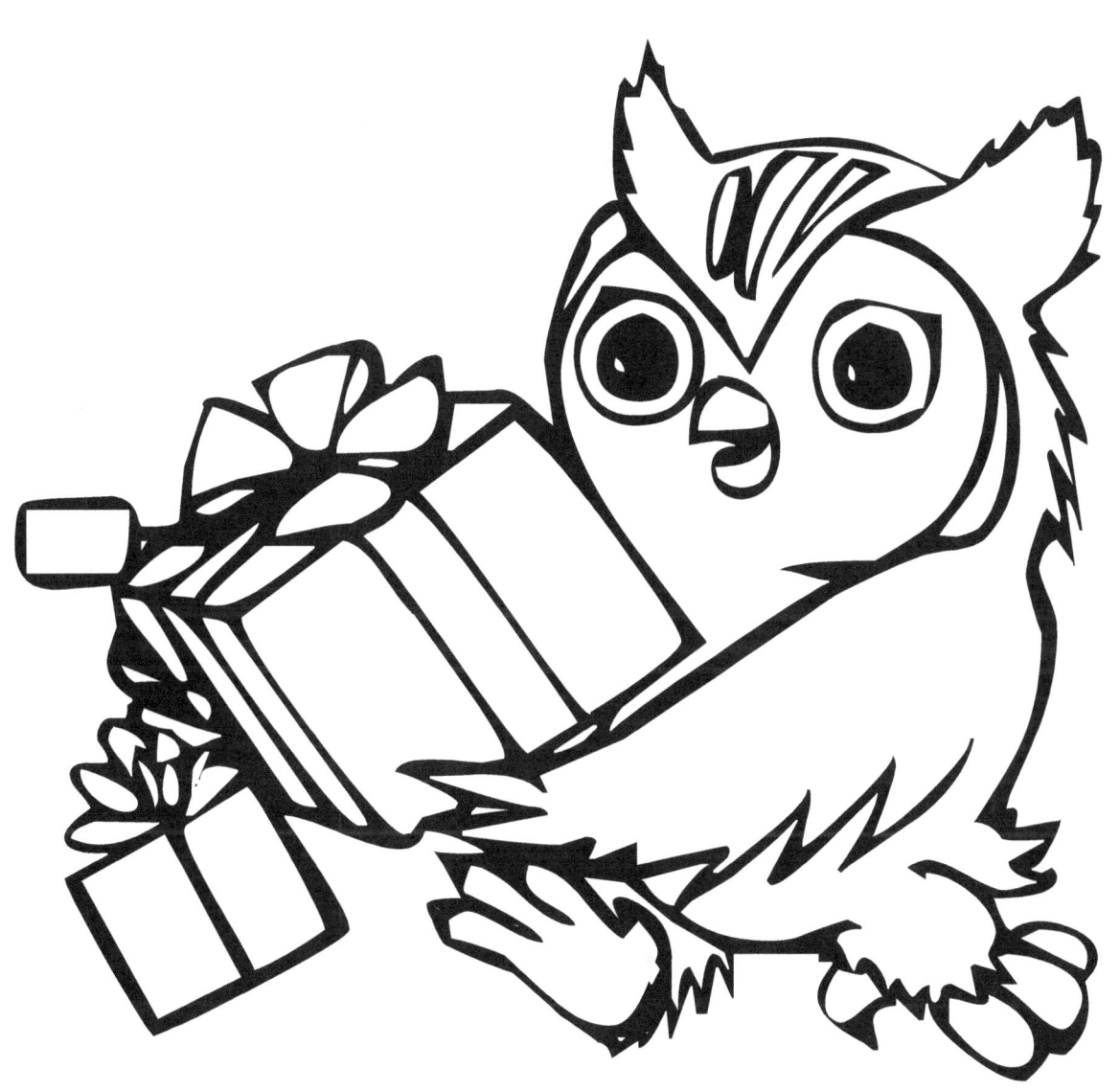

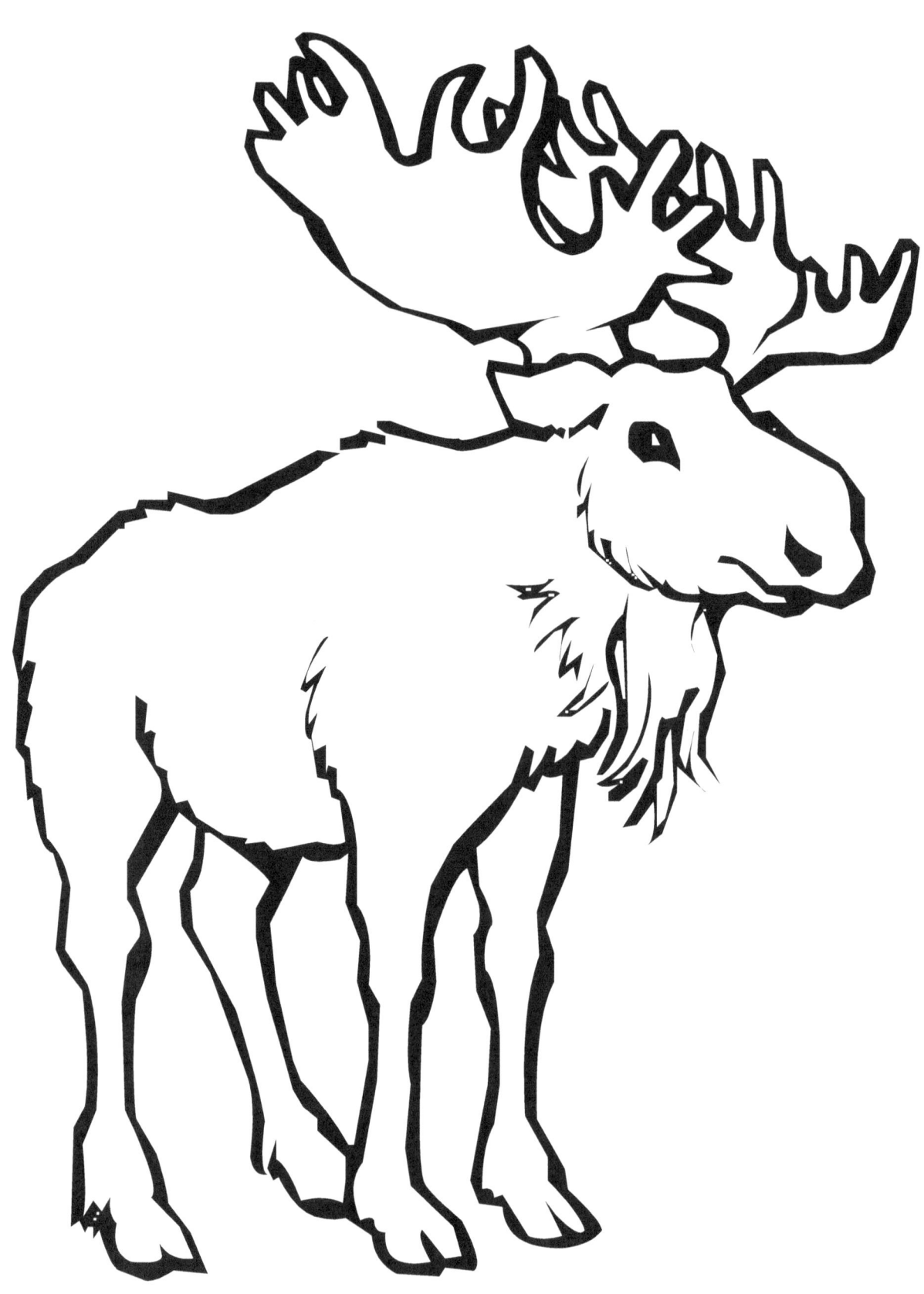

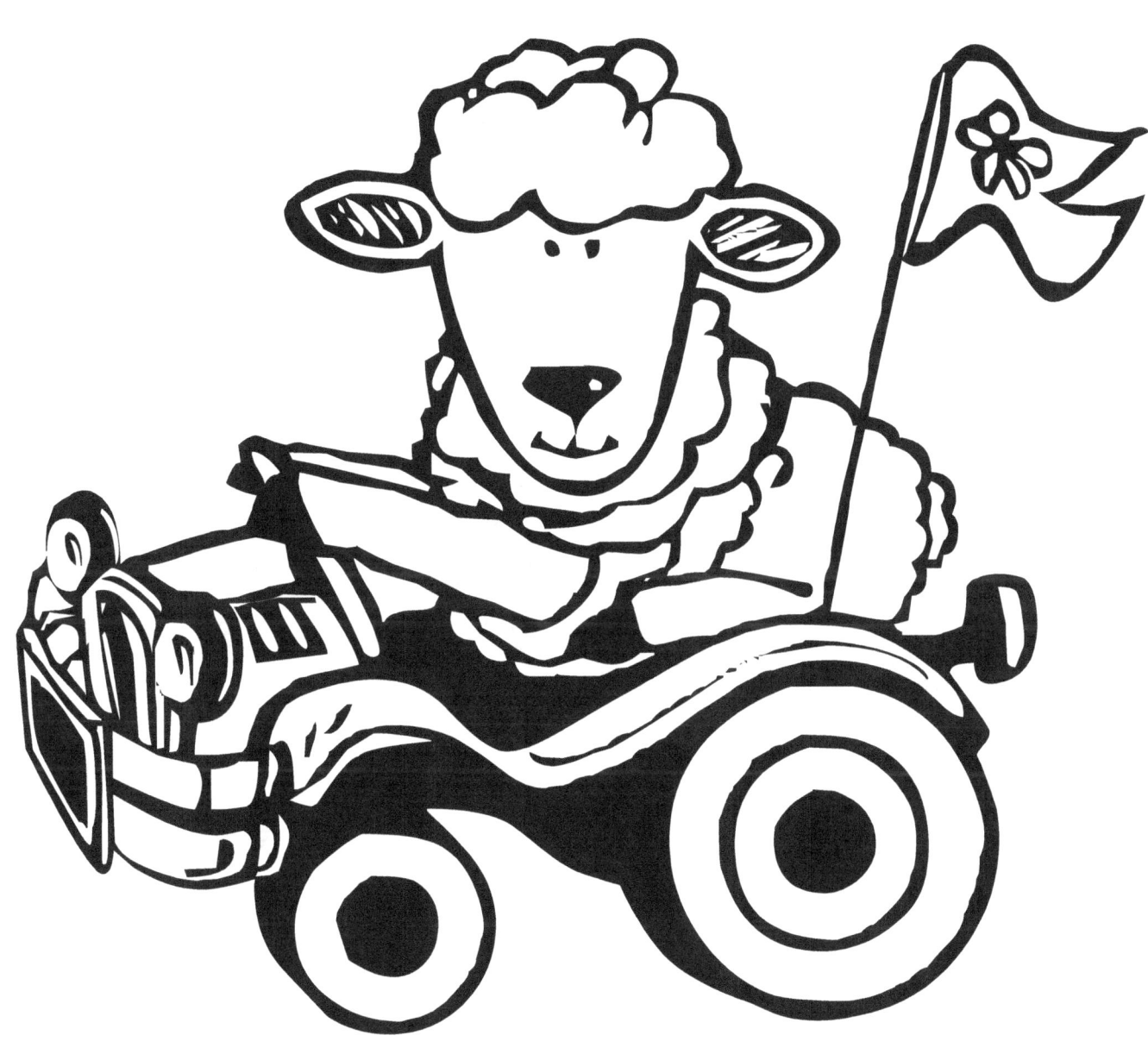

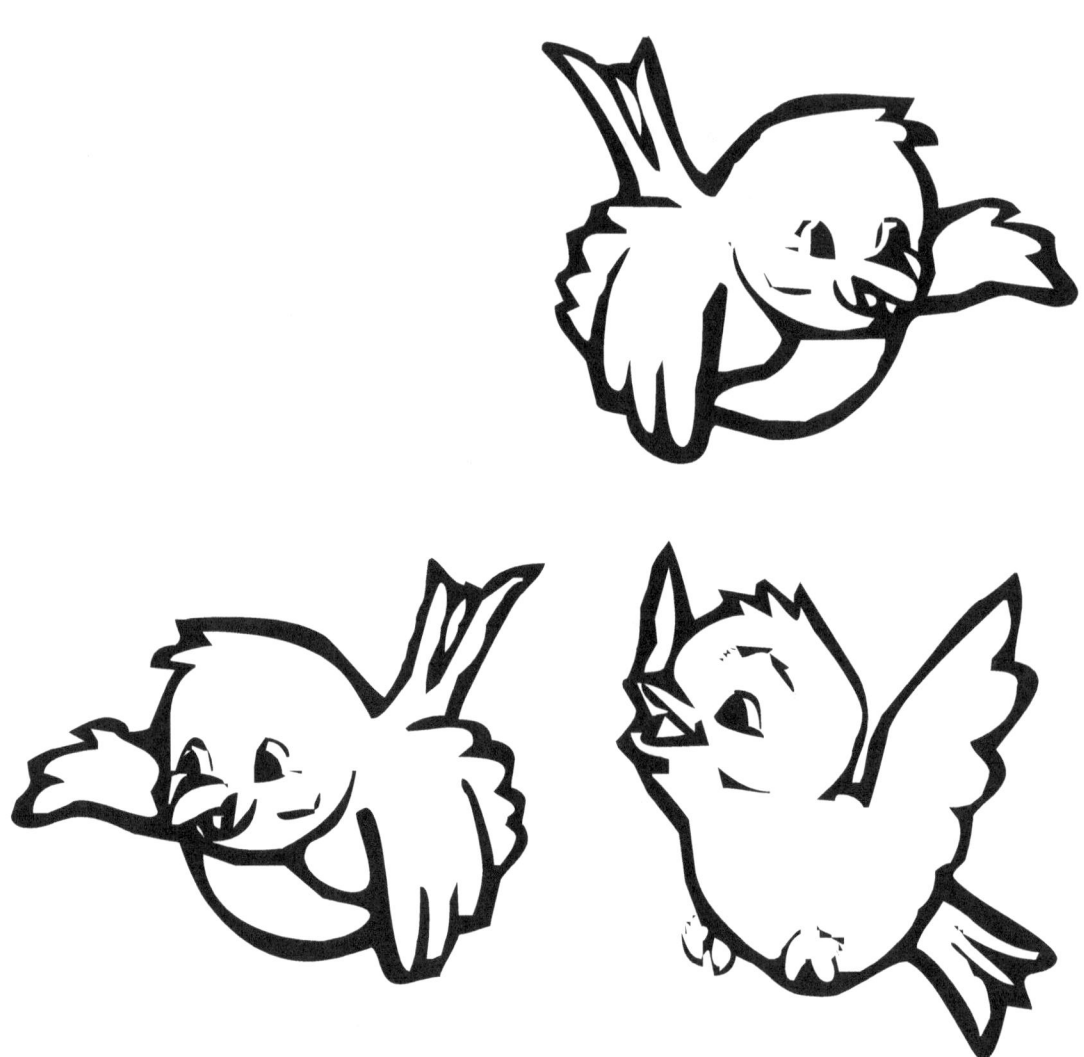

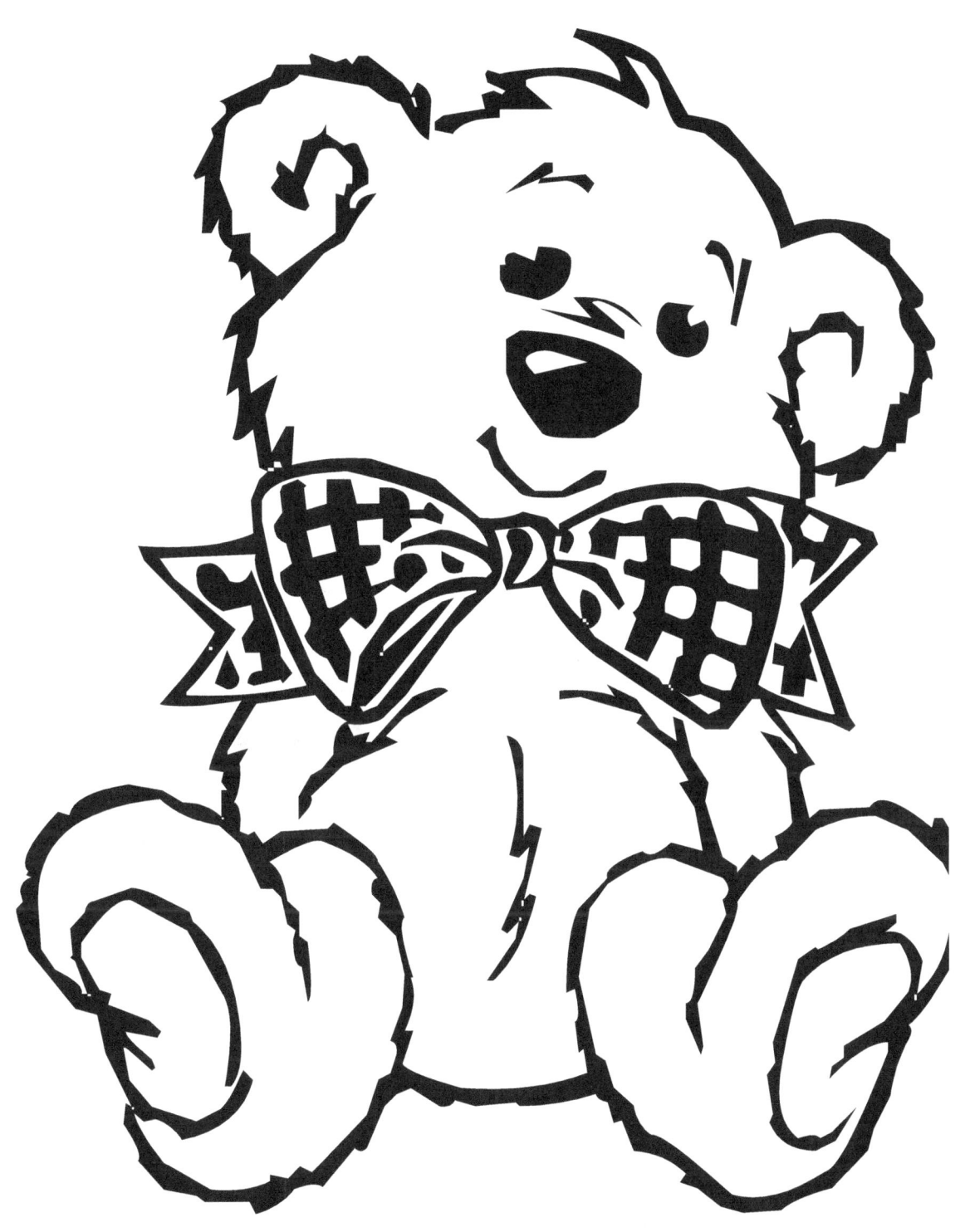

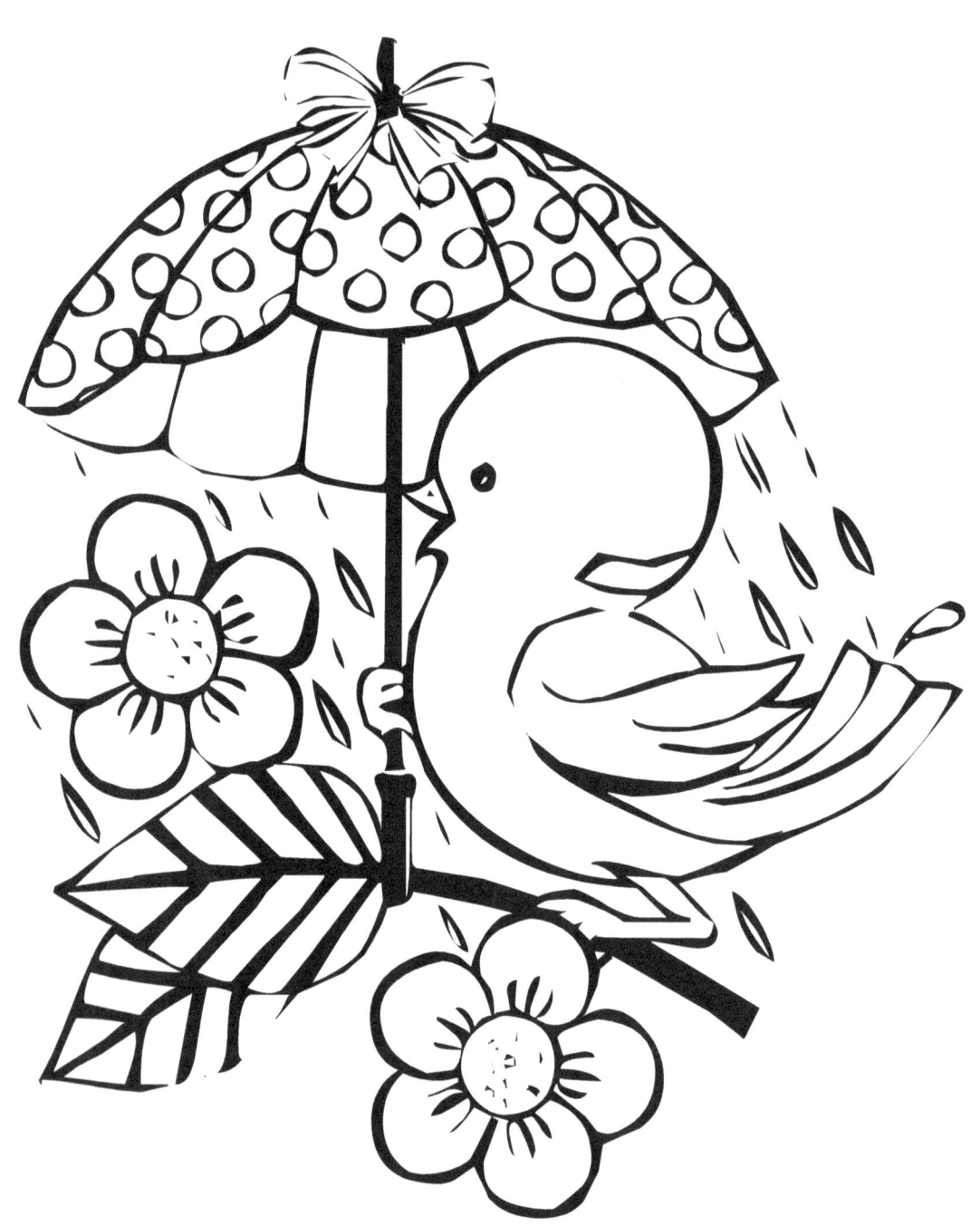

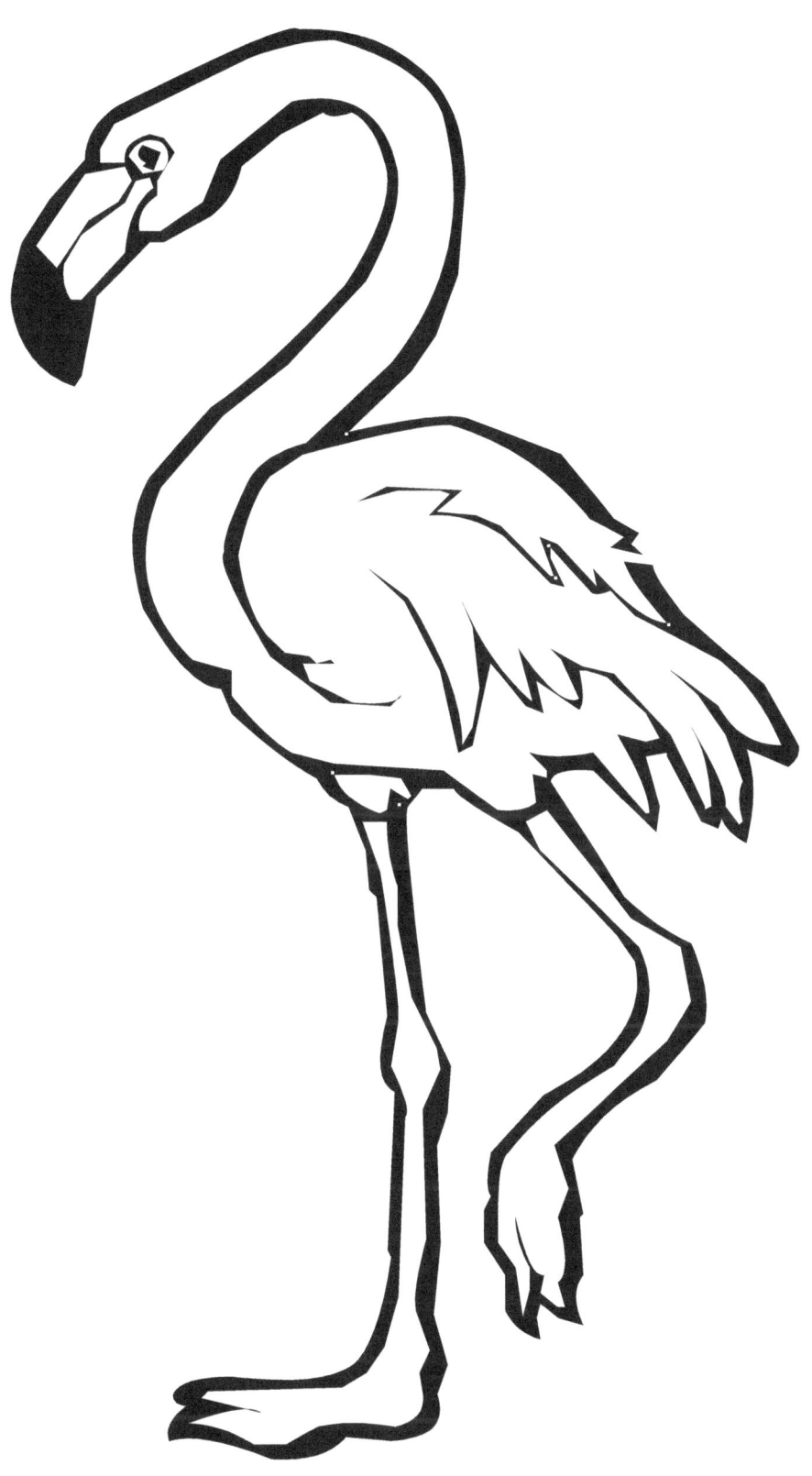

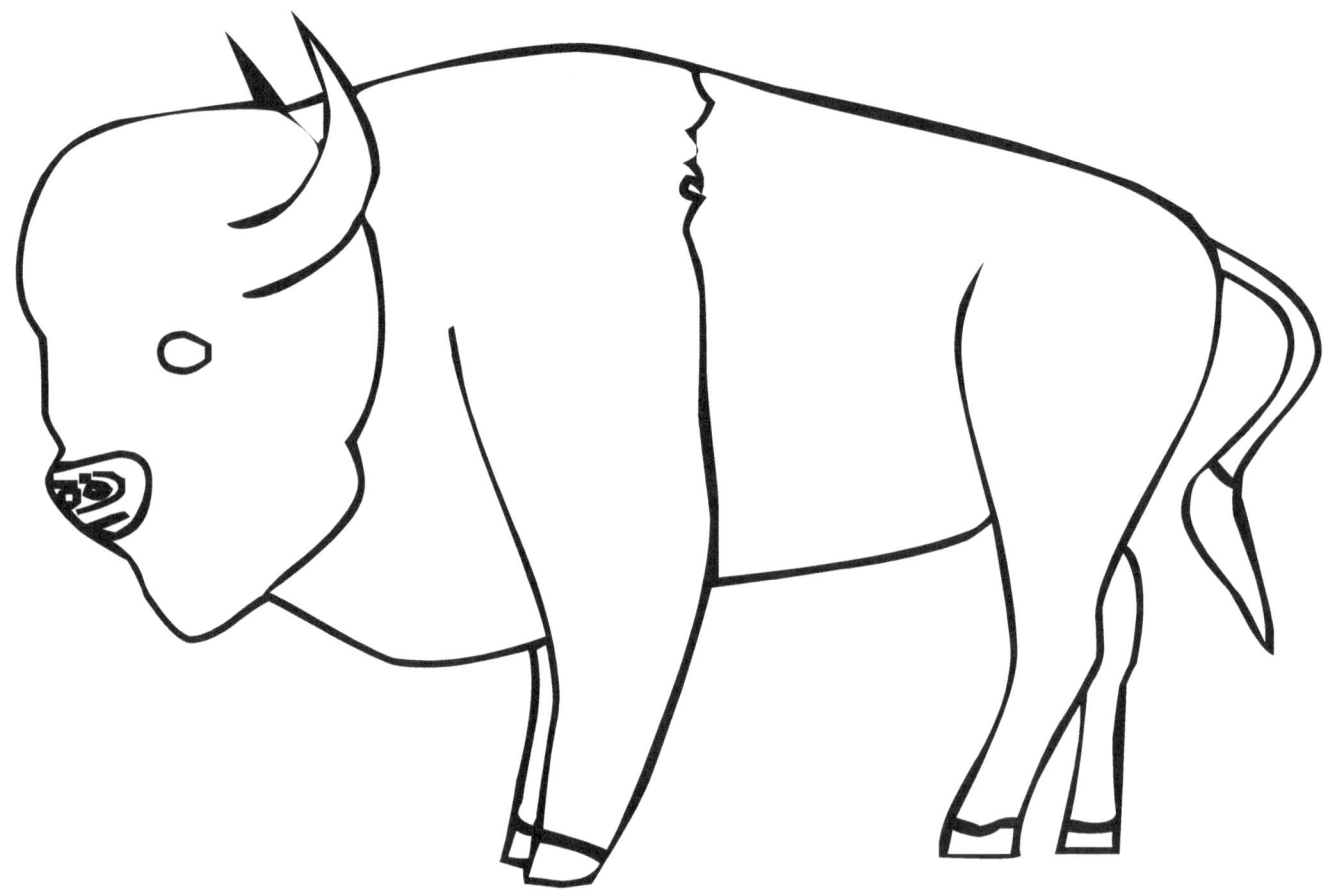

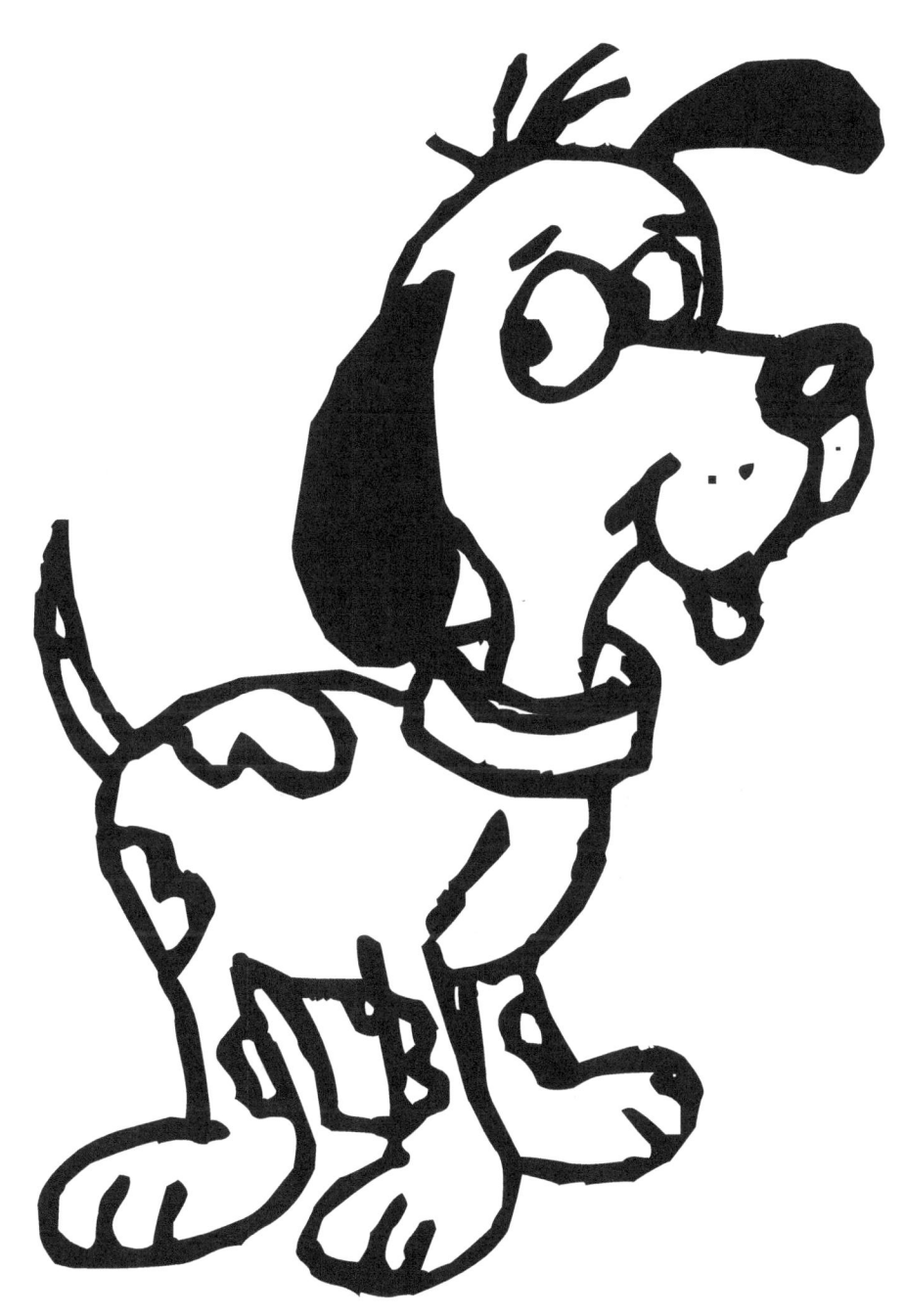

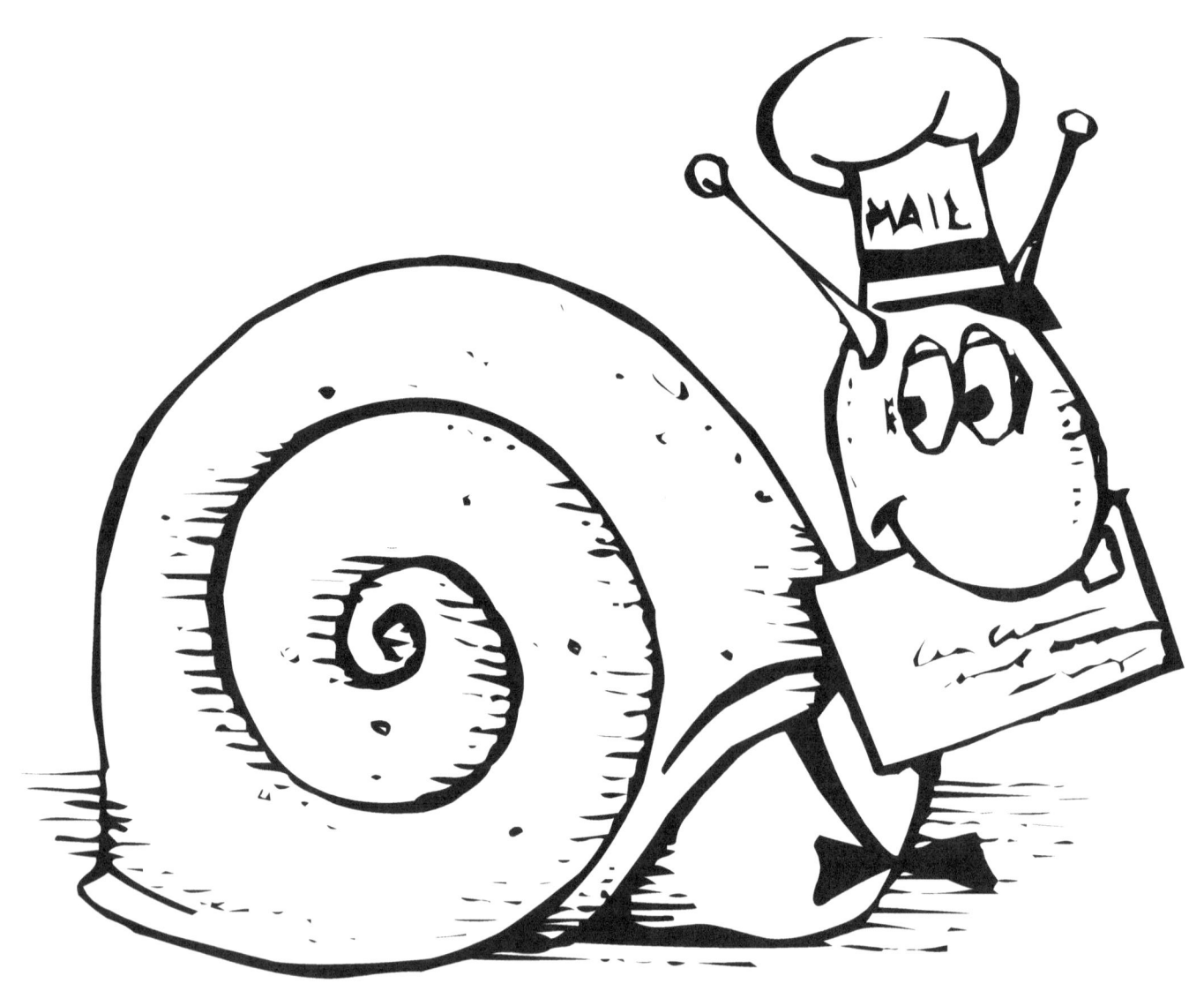

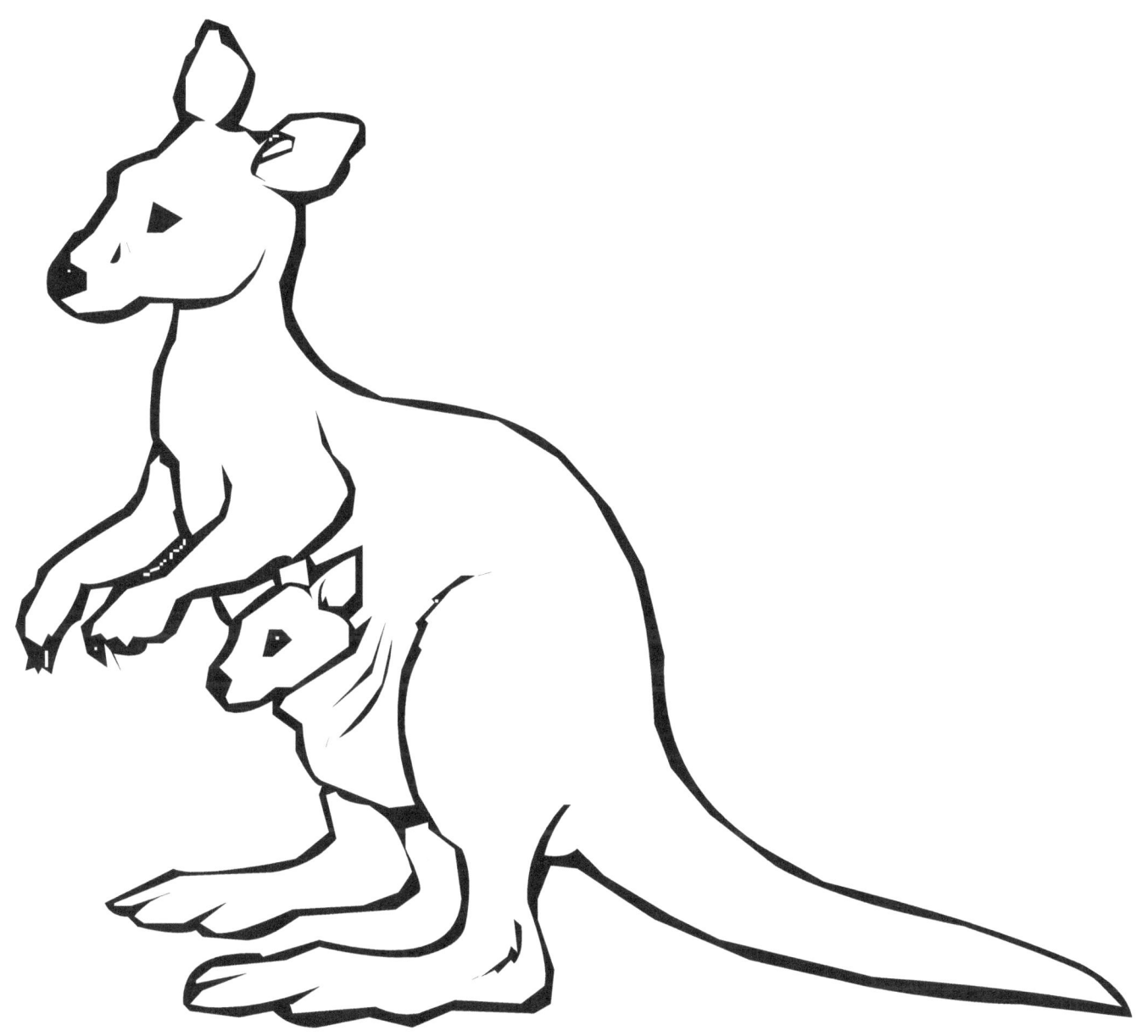

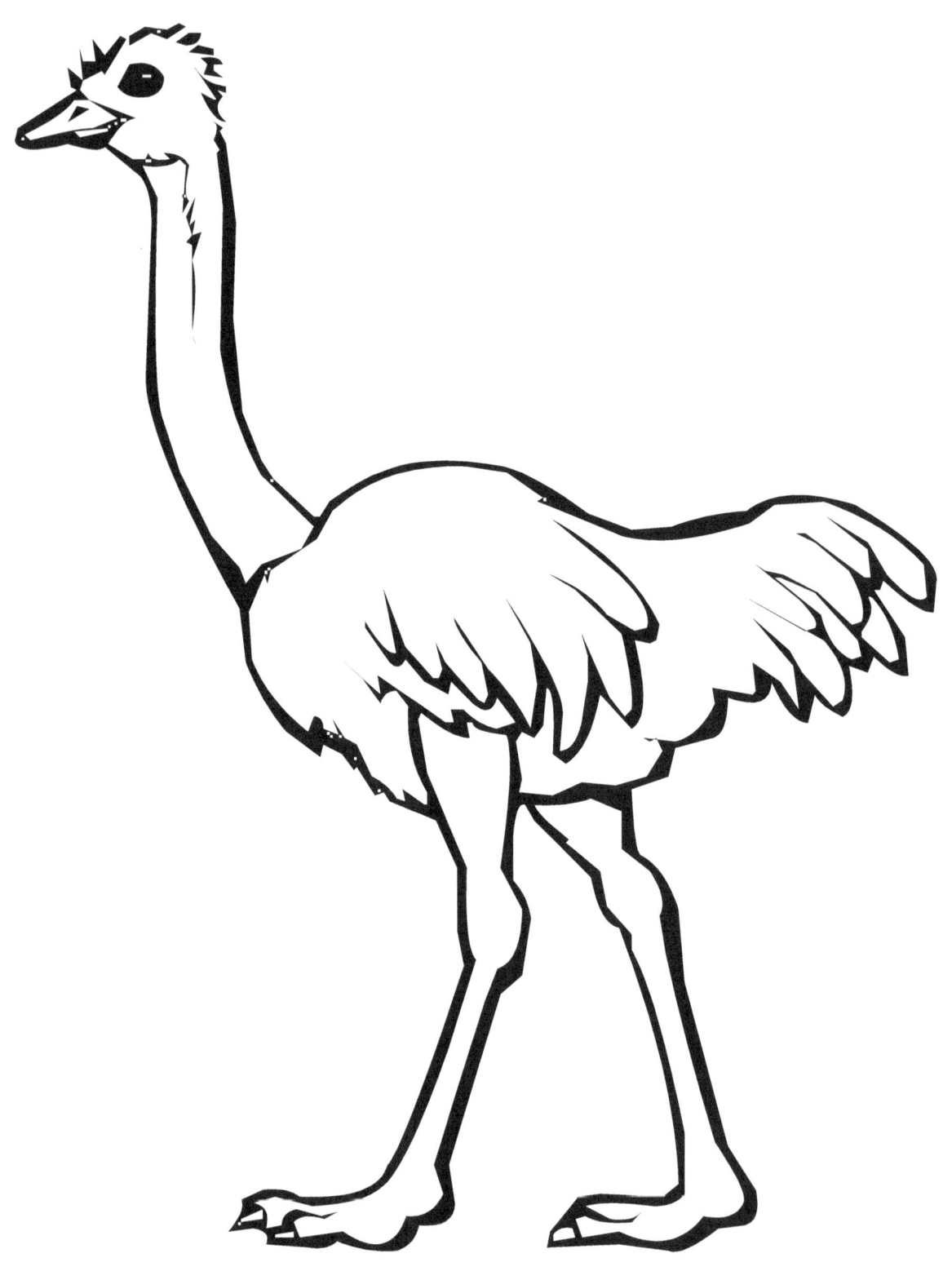

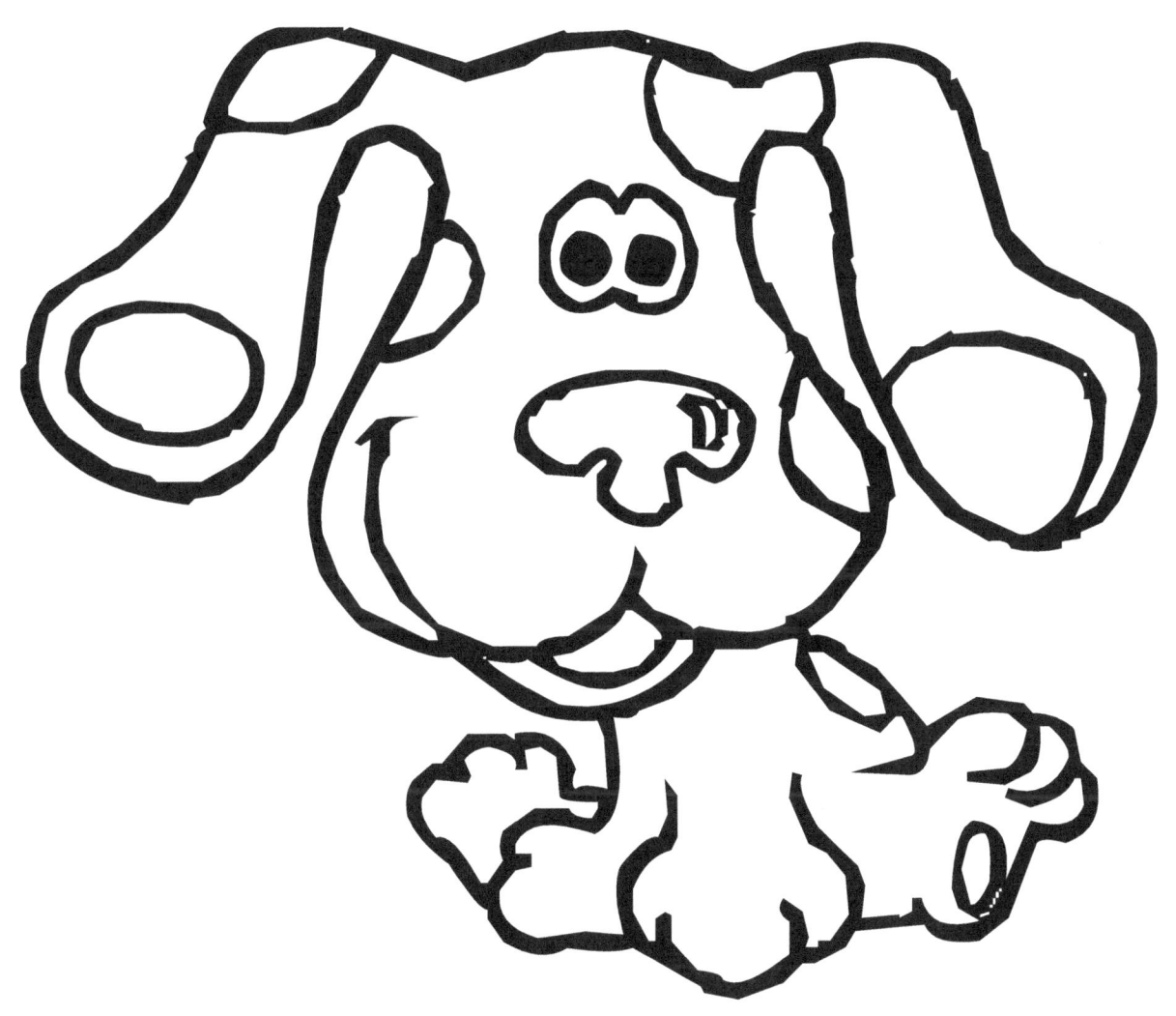

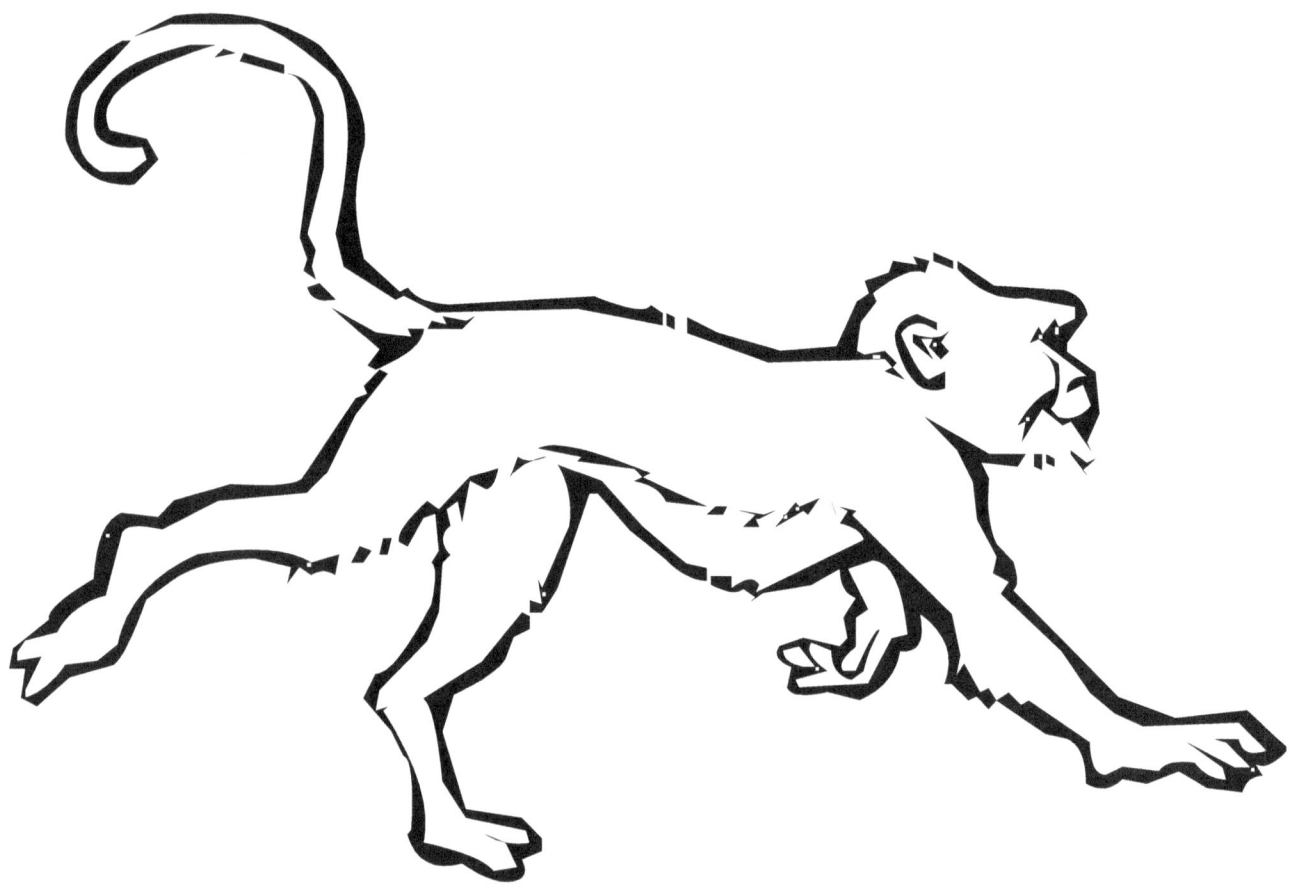

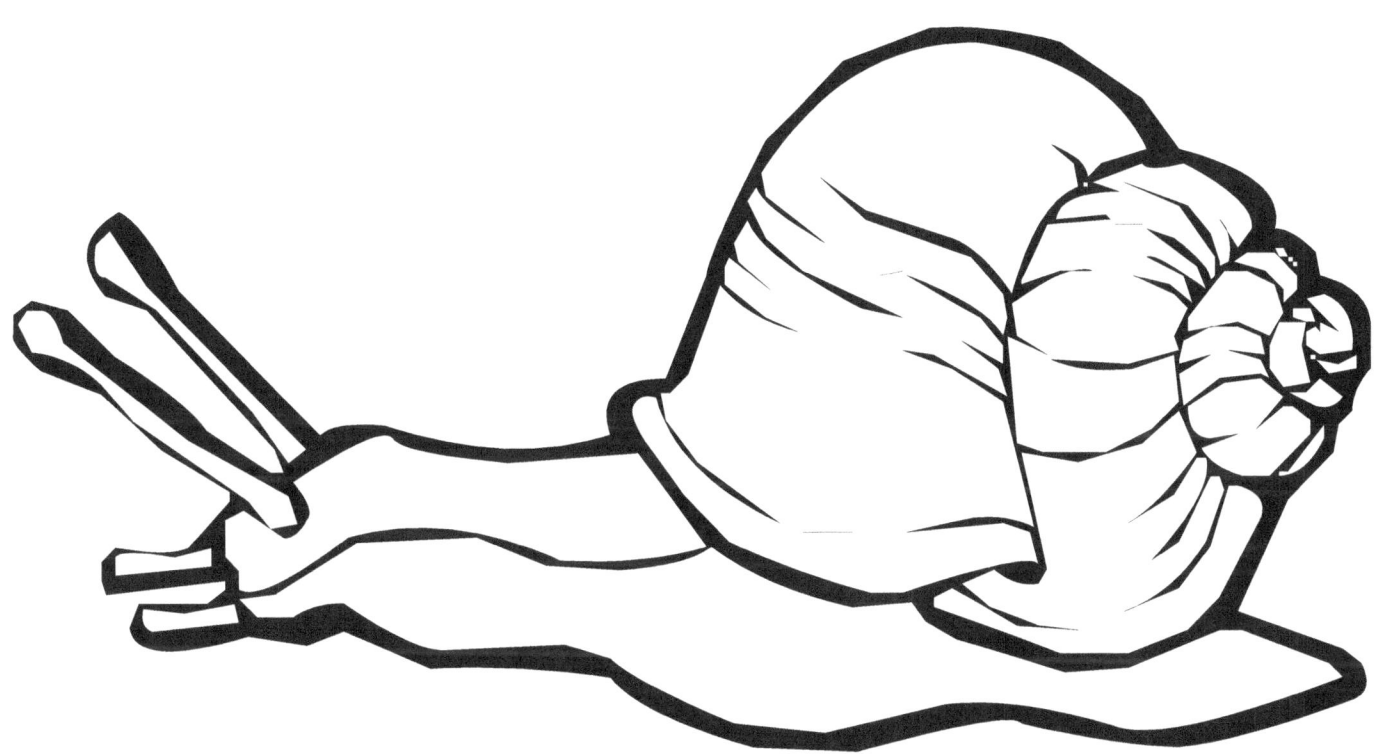

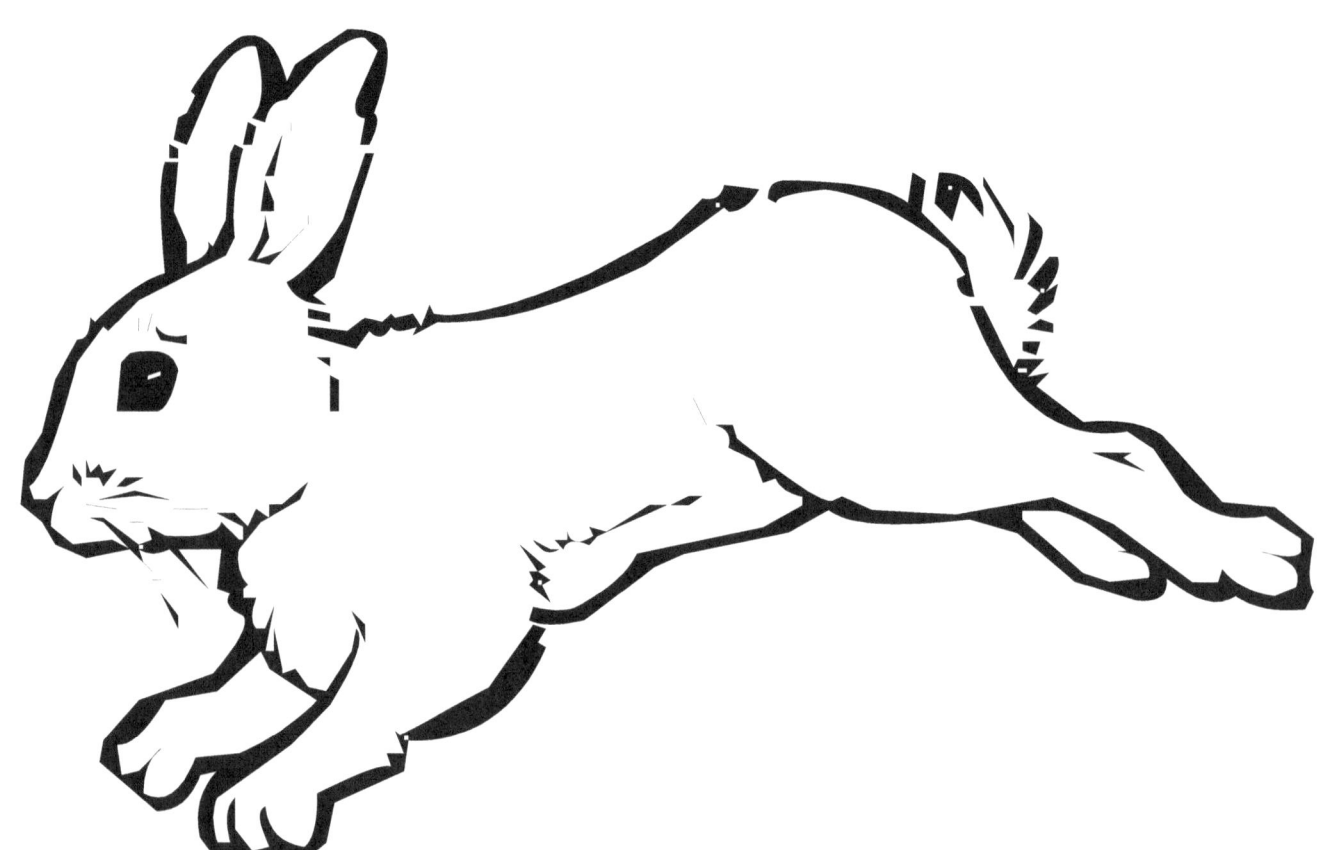

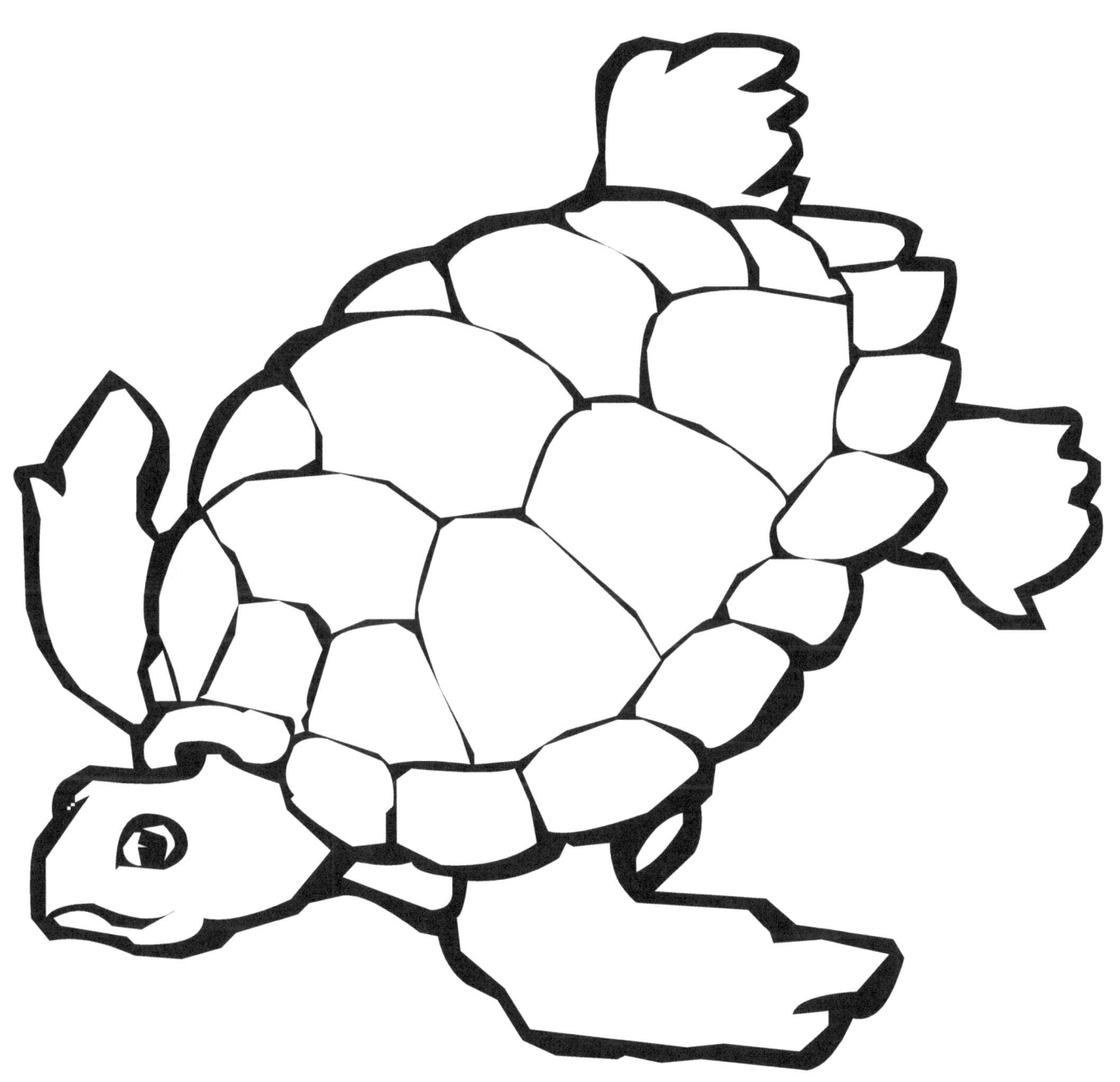

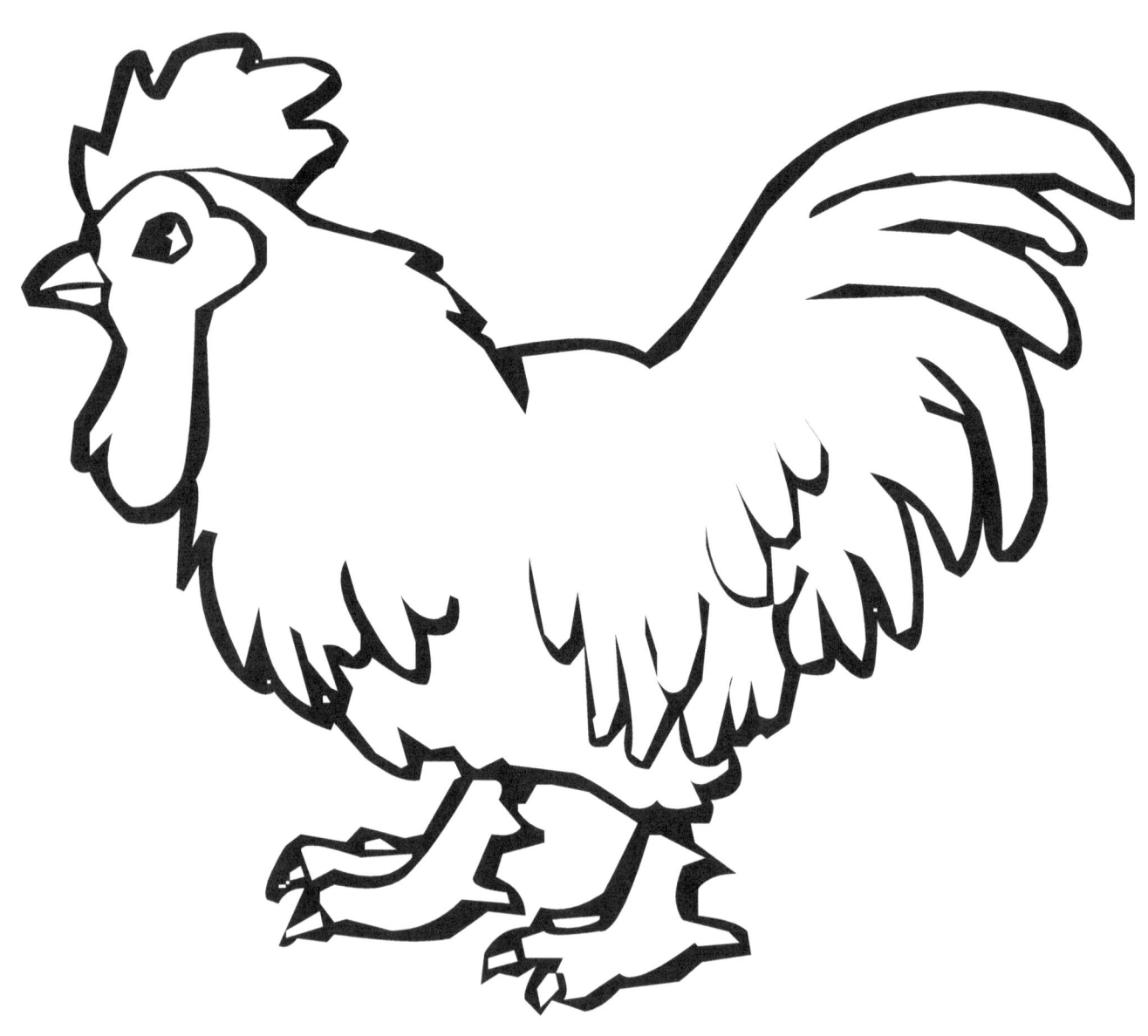

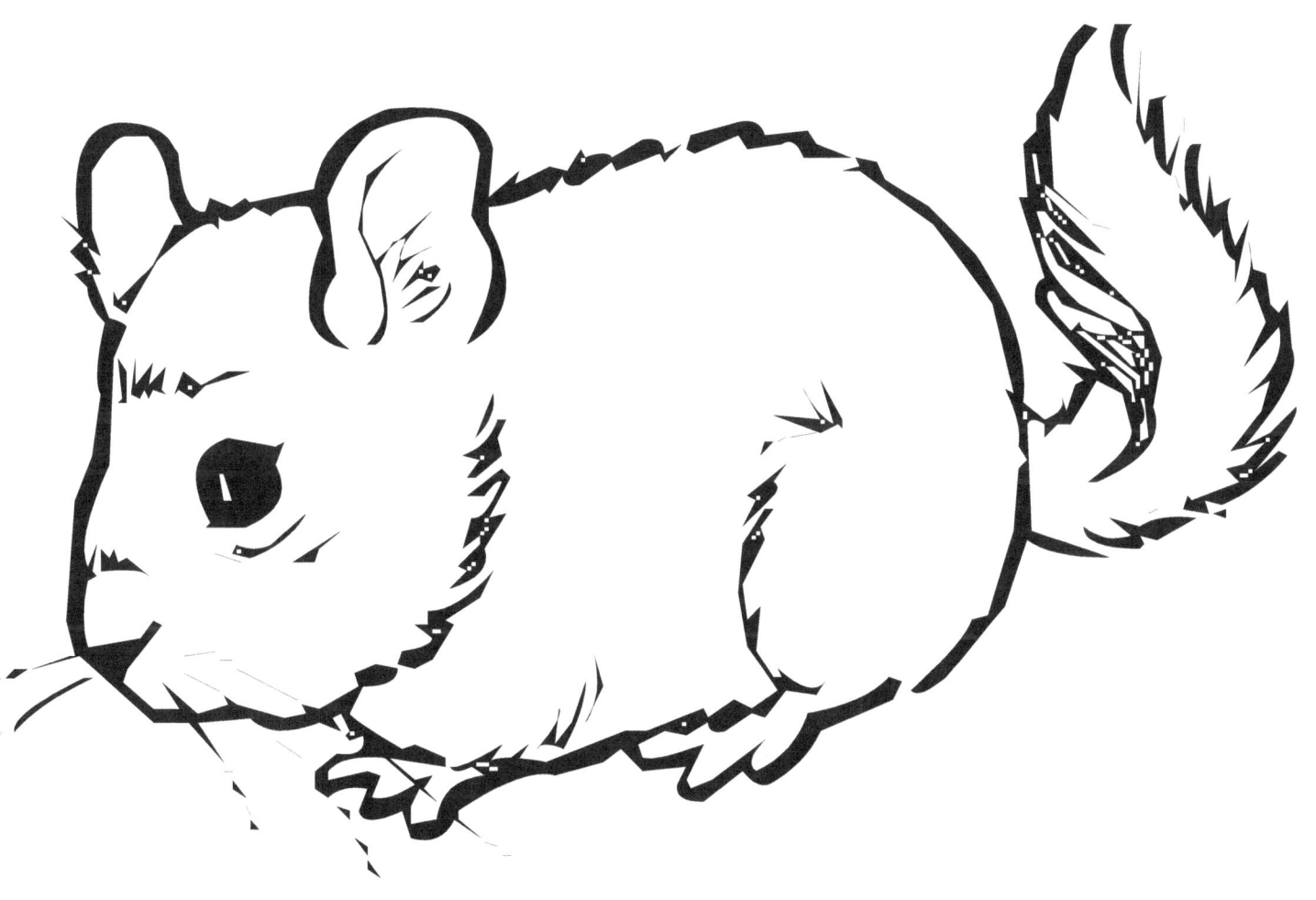

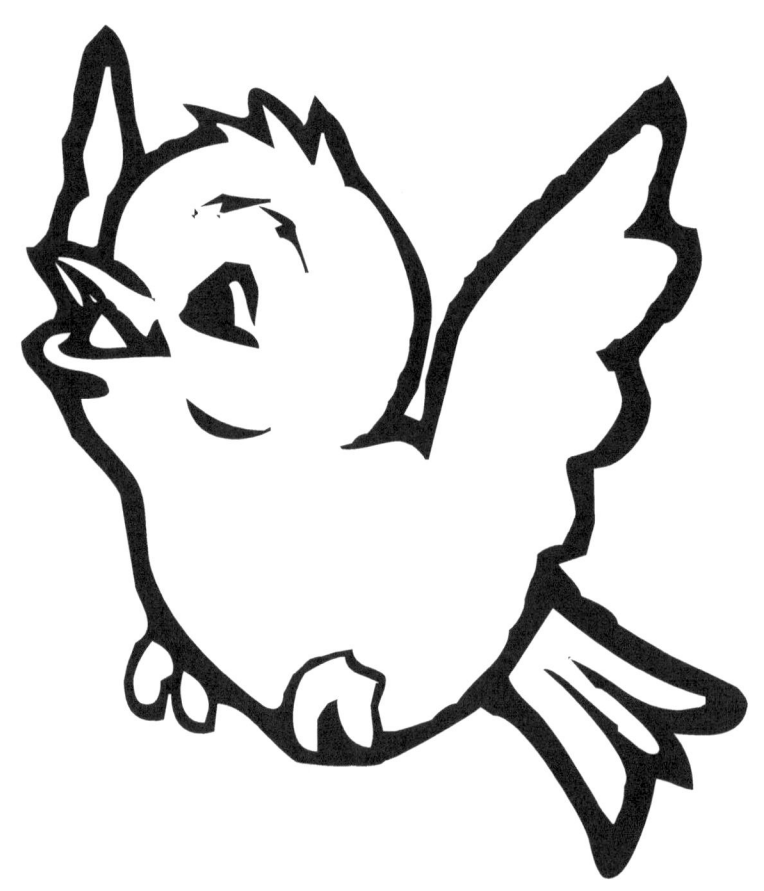

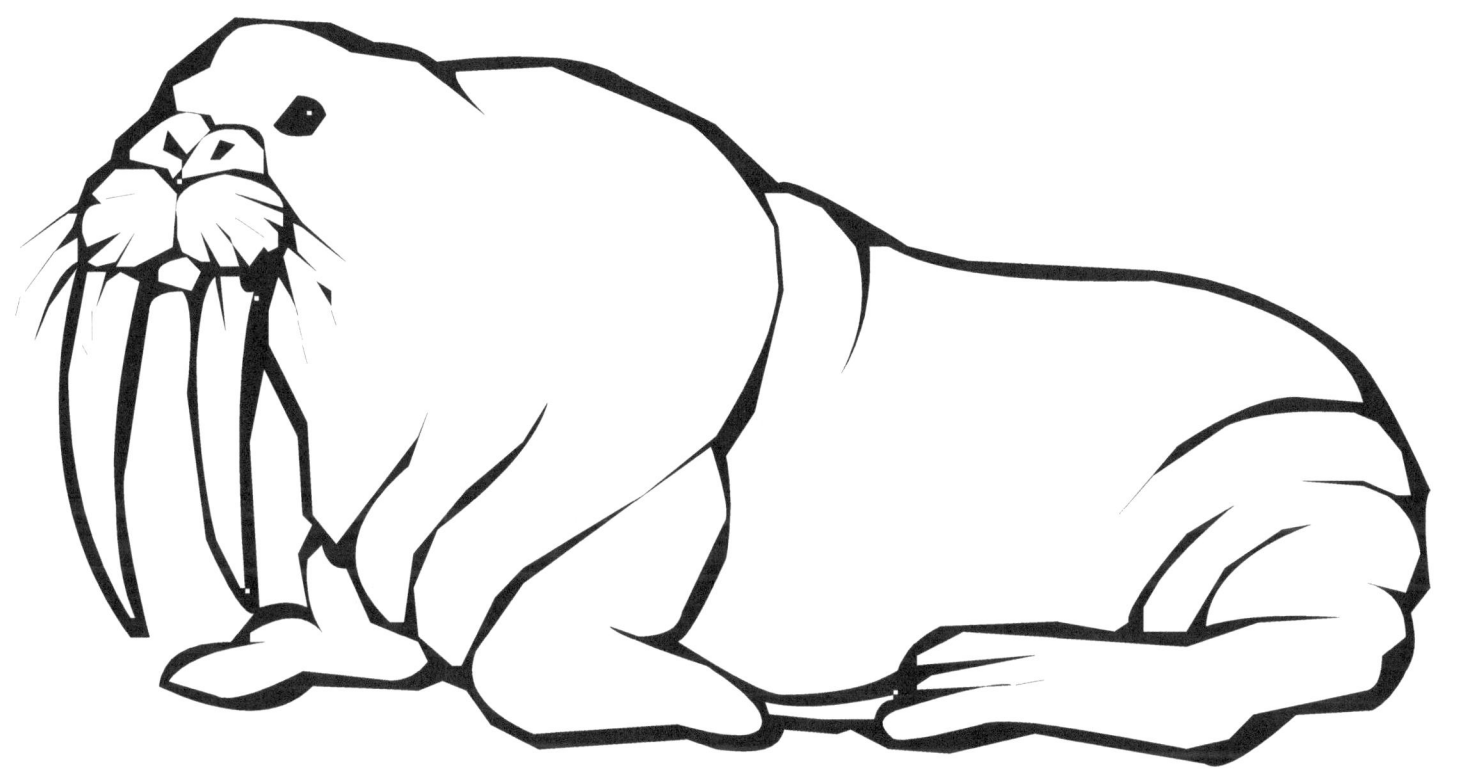

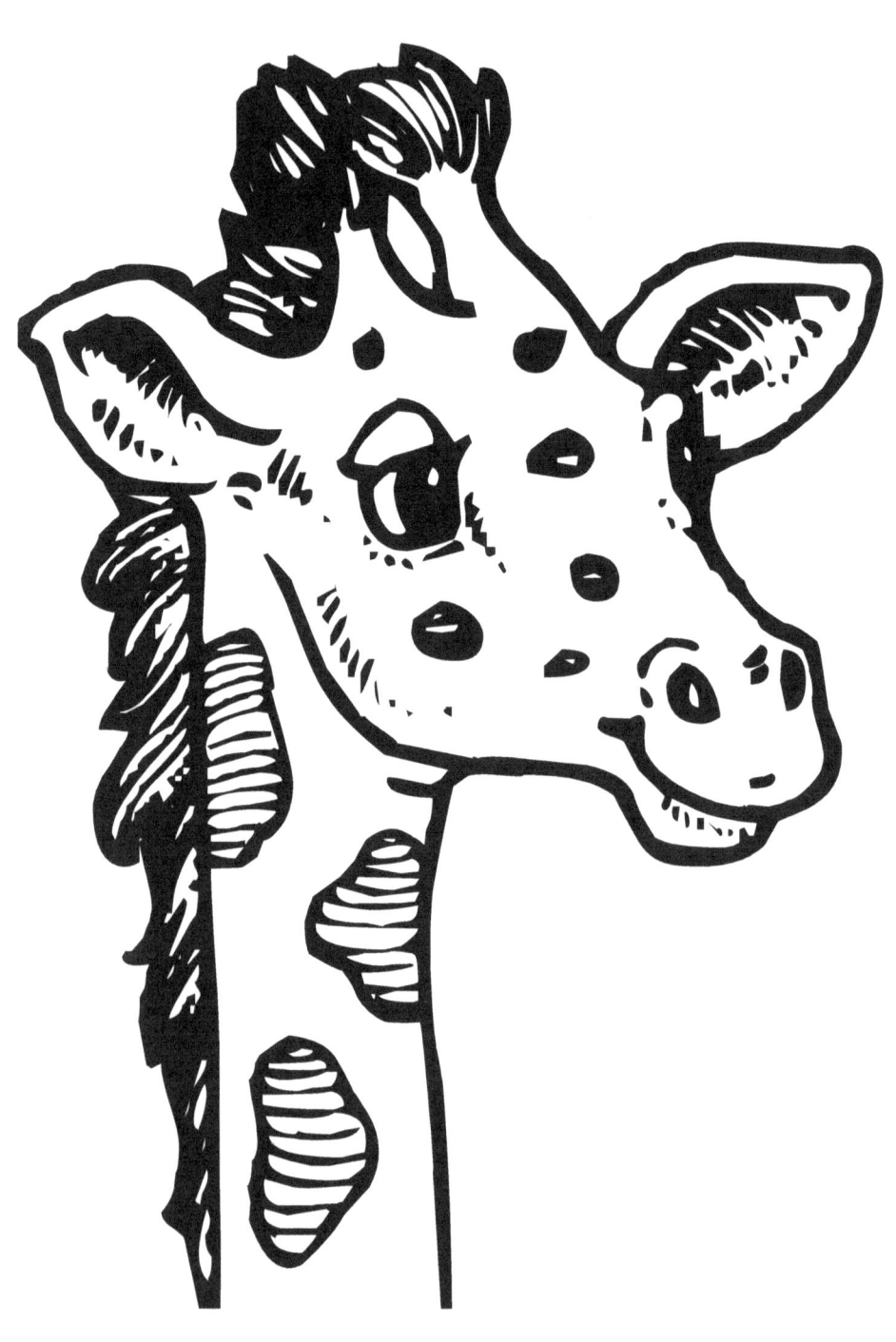

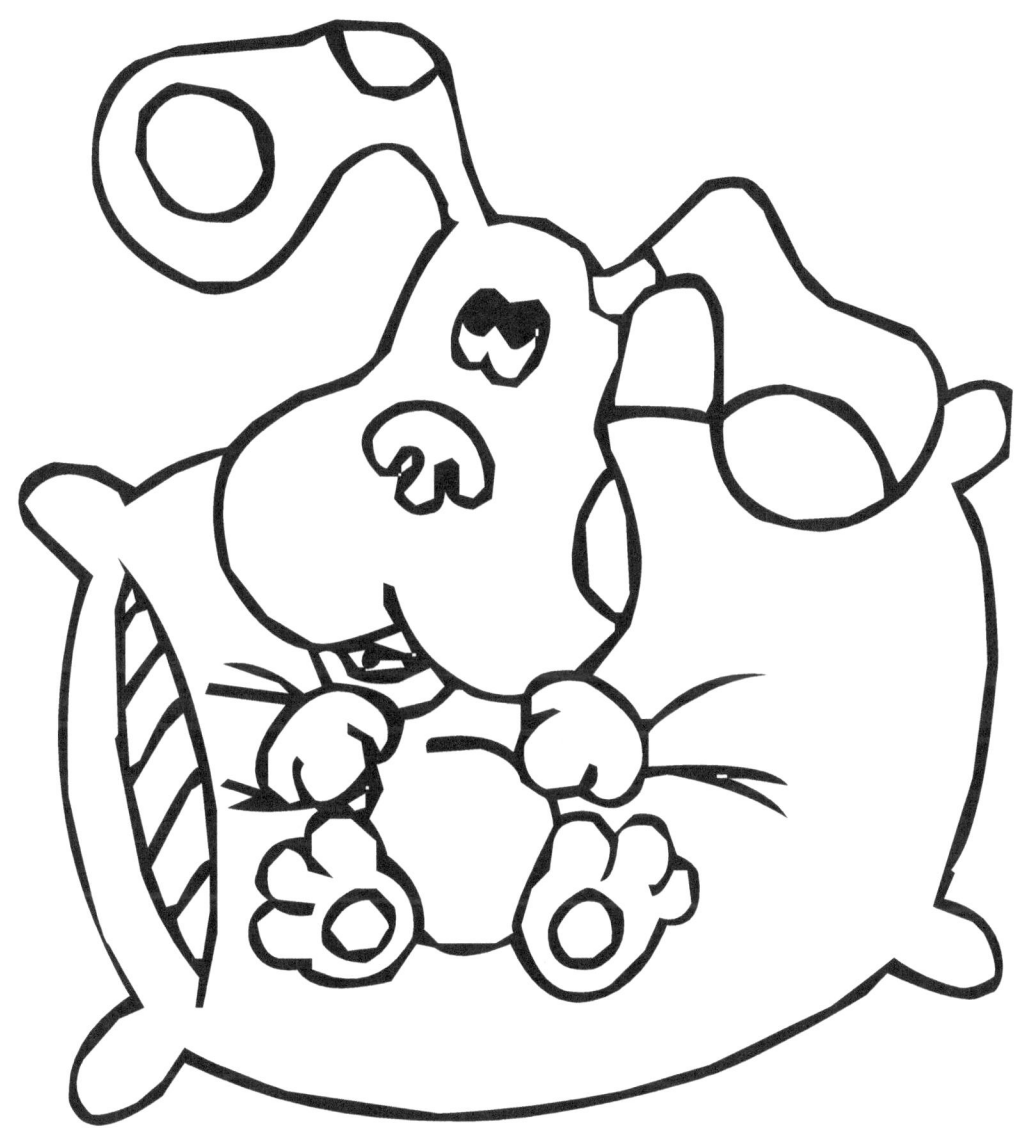

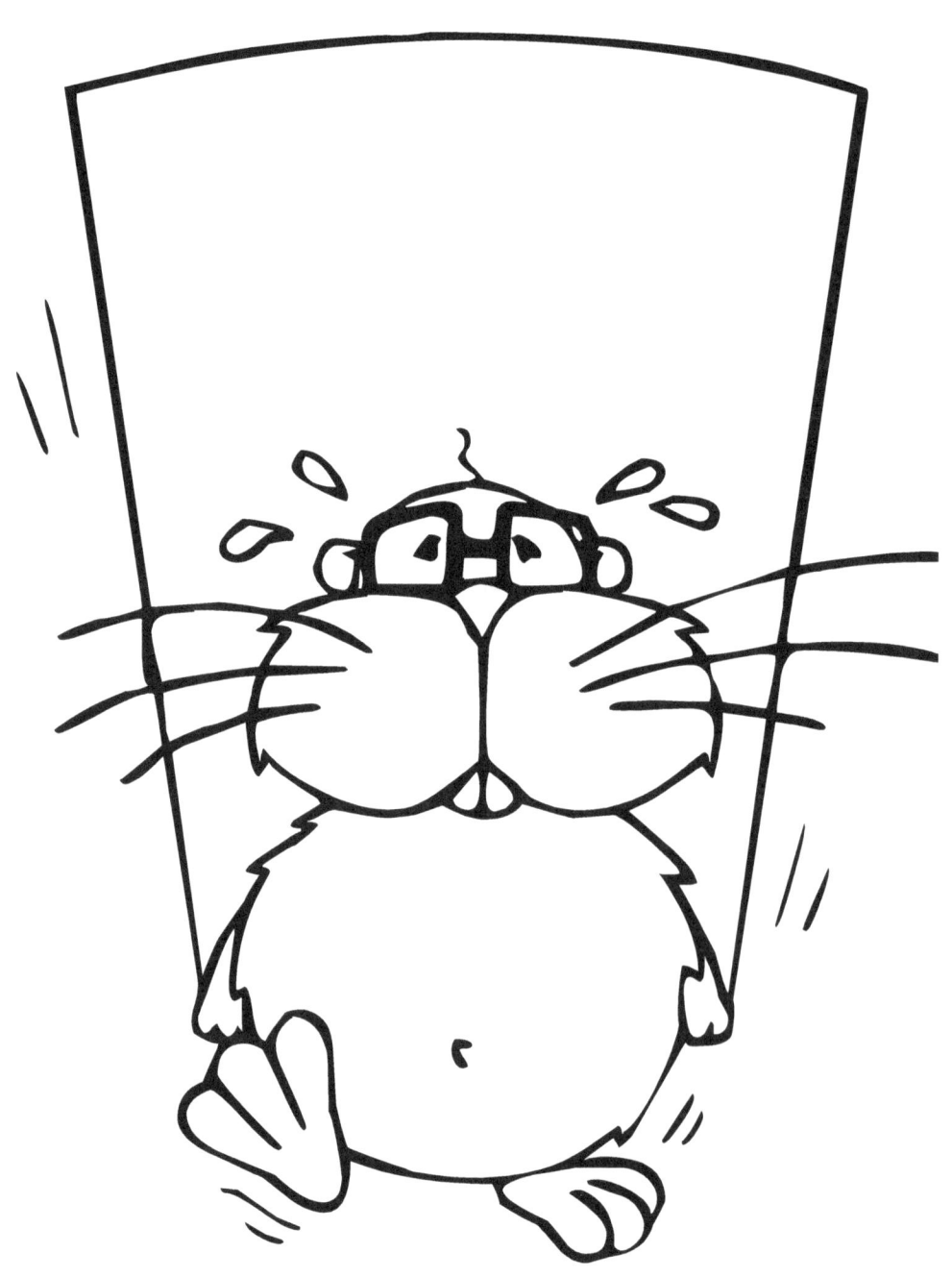

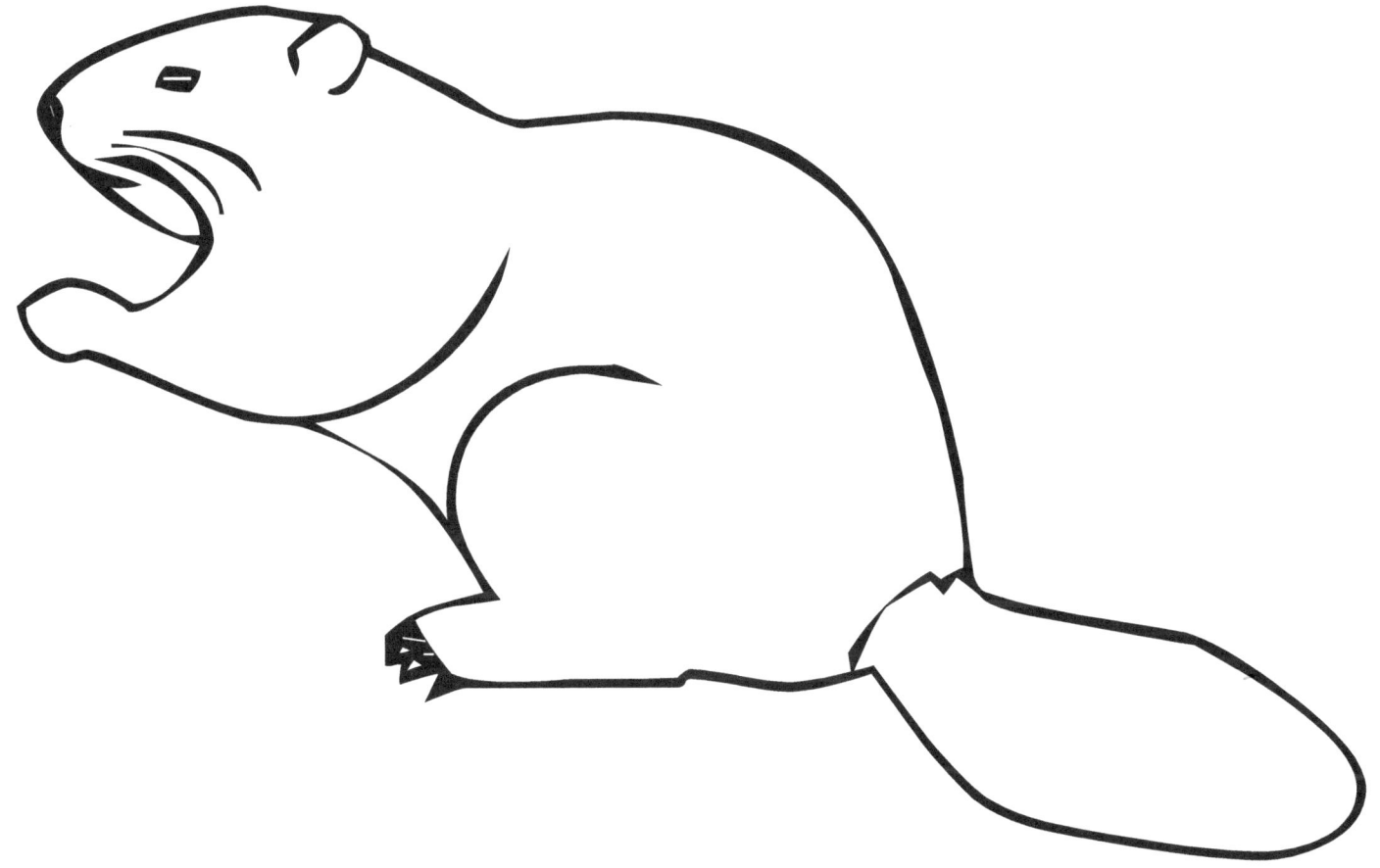

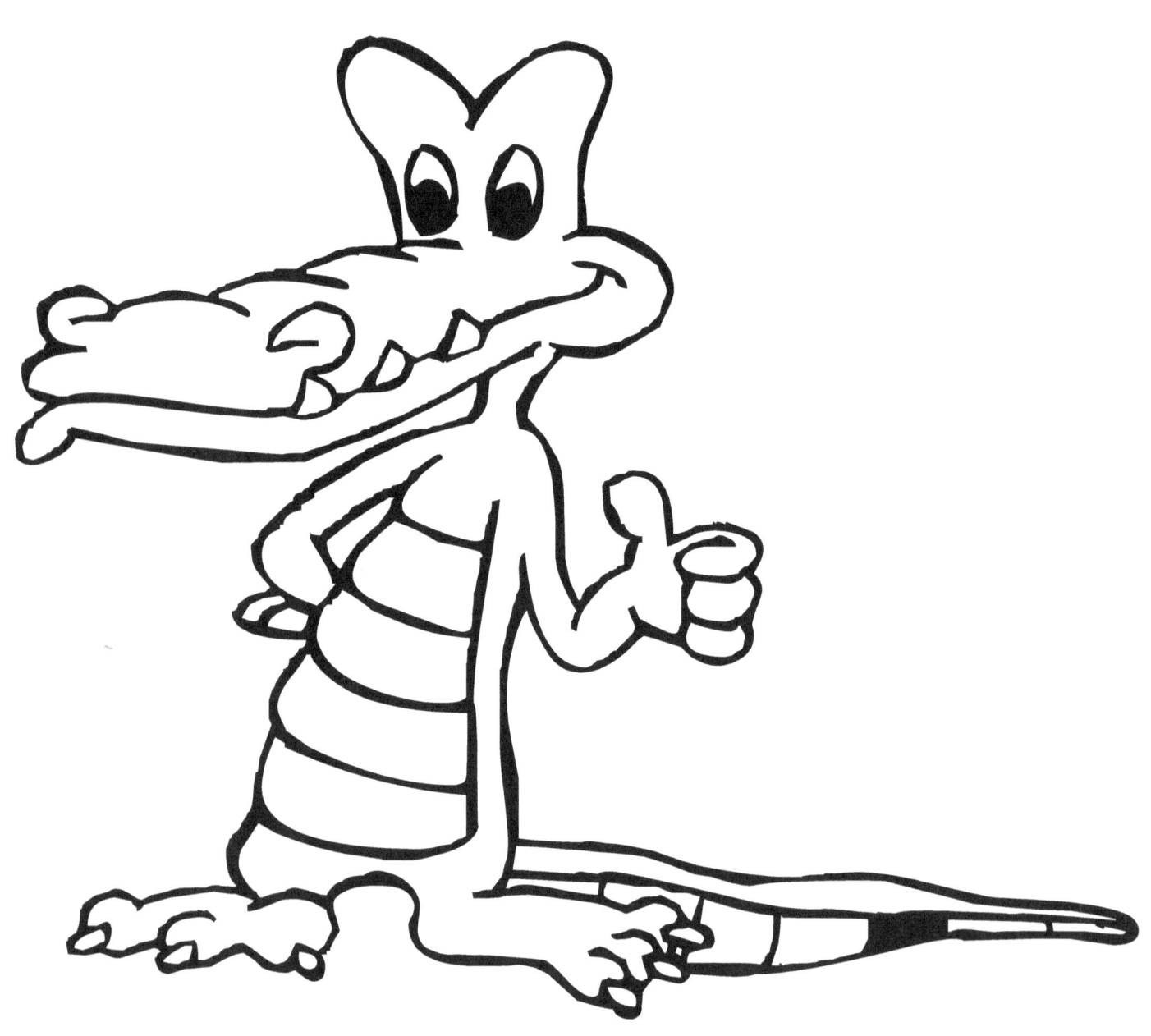

Draw Your Favourite Picture Here

Intentionally Left Blank

Test Your Colors Now

Intentionally Left Blank

www.ingramcontent.com/pod-product-compliance
Lightning Source LLC
Chambersburg PA
CBHW081014170526

45158CB00010B/3039